Nick Vandome

macOS Catalina

for all Macs (iMac, Mac mini, Mac Pro and MacBook)
with macOS Catalina (v 10.15)

In easy steps is an imprint of In Easy Steps Limited
16 Hamilton Terrace · Holly Walk · Leamington Spa
Warwickshire · United Kingdom · CV32 4LY
www.ineasysteps.com

Notice of Liability
Every effort has been made to ensure that this book contains accurate
and current information. However, In Easy Steps Limited and the
author shall not be liable for any loss or damage suffered by readers
as a result of any information contained herein.

Trademarks
OS X® and macOS® are registered trademarks of Apple Computer
Inc. All other trademarks are acknowledged as belonging to their
respective companies.

In Easy Steps Limited supports The Forest Stewardship Council (FSC),
the leading international forest certification organization. All our titles
that are printed on Greenpeace approved FSC certified paper carry the
FSC logo.

MIX
Paper from
responsible sources
FSC® C020837

Printed and bound in the United Kingdom

ISBN 978-1-84078-864-8

Contents

1 Introducing macOS Catalina

macOS Catalina is the latest operating system from Apple, for its range of desktop and laptop computers. This chapter introduces macOS Catalina, showing how to install it and get started using its array of features including the digital voice assistant, Siri, and Dark Mode for changing the color of items.

About macOS Catalina

UNIX is an operating system that has traditionally been used for large commercial mainframe computers. It is renowned for its stability and ability to be used within different computing environments.

The Apple Pencil can now be used on Mac computers with macOS Catalina to perform tasks such as drawing and sketching, in compatible apps, and marking up screenshots and PDF documents.

The New icon pictured above indicates a new or enhanced feature introduced with the latest version of macOS – macOS Catalina.

macOS Catalina is the 15th version (10.15) of the operating system for Apple computers: the iMac, MacBook, Mac mini and Mac Pro. Although it is still a development of the OS X (pronounced "ten") operating system for Macs, the naming convention was changed to macOS in 2016, to more clearly identify it as belonging to the Mac, rather than a mobile device such as the iPad or iPhone. Like earlier versions, it is based on the UNIX programming language, which is a very stable and secure operating environment, and this ensures that macOS is one of the most stable consumer operating systems that has ever been designed. More importantly for the user, it is also one of the most stylish and user-friendly operating systems available.

macOS Catalina continues the functionality of several of its Mac operating system predecessors, including using some of the functionality that is available on Apple's mobile devices such as the iPad and the iPhone. The three main areas where the functionality of the mobile devices has been incorporated into the desktop and laptop operating system are:

- The way apps can be downloaded and installed. Instead of using a disc, macOS Catalina utilizes the App Store to provide apps, which can be installed in a couple of steps.

- Options for navigating around pages and applications on a trackpad or a Magic Mouse. Instead of having to use a mouse or a traditional laptop trackpad, macOS Catalina uses Multi-Touch Gestures for navigating apps and web pages.

- Siri, Apple's digital voice assistant, has now made the transition from being only available on mobile devices to being included with macOS Catalina too.

macOS Catalina continues the evolution of the operating system, by adding features and enhancing existing ones. These include:

- The replacement of the iTunes app with three dedicated apps: Music, TV and Podcasts.

- Updates to existing apps, including Photos, Reminders, Notes and Safari.

- The inclusion of Screen Time for monitoring screen usage and also controlling access to apps and specific content.

Installing macOS Catalina

When it comes to installing macOS Catalina you do not need to worry about an installation CD or DVD; it can be downloaded and installed directly from the online App Store. New Macs will have macOS Catalina installed. The following range is compatible with macOS Catalina, and can be upgraded with it, directly from the App Store:

- iMac (Mid 2012 or newer).
- iMac Pro (2017).
- MacBook (Early 2015 or newer).
- MacBook Pro (Mid 2012 or newer).
- MacBook Air (Mid 2012 or newer).
- Mac mini (Late 2012 or newer).
- Mac Pro (Late 2013 or newer).

If you want to install macOS Catalina on an existing Mac, you will need to have the minimum requirements of:

- OS X 8 or later.
- 2GB of memory.
- 12.5GB of available storage for installation.

If your Mac meets these requirements, you can download and install macOS Catalina, for free, as follows:

1. Click on this icon on the Dock to access the App Store (or select **Software Update...**; see tip)

2. Locate the **macOS Catalina** icon using the App Store Search box

3. Click on the **Get** button and follow the installation instructions

macOS Catalina is a new version of the Mac operating system. It contains a number of enhancements to make the operating system faster and more reliable than ever.

To check your computer's software version and upgrade options, click on **Apple menu** > **About This Mac** from the main Menu bar. Click on the **Overview** tab and click on the **Software Update...** button. See page 13 for details.

The macOS Environment

The first most noticeable element about macOS is its elegant user interface. This has been designed to create a user-friendly graphic overlay to the UNIX operating system at the heart of macOS, and it is a combination of rich colors and sharp, original graphics. The main elements that make up the initial macOS environment are:

Apple menu   Menu bar   Windows   Menu bar icons

The Dock   Desktop

The Dock is designed to help make organizing and opening items as quick and easy as possible. For a detailed look at the Dock, see Chapter 2.

Many of the behind-the-scenes features of macOS Catalina are aimed at saving power on your Mac. These include timer-coalescing technologies for saving processing and battery power; features for saving energy when apps are not being used; power-saving features in Safari for ignoring additional content provided by web page plug-ins; and memory compression to make your Mac quicker and more responsive.

The **Apple menu** is standardized throughout macOS, regardless of the app in use.

Menus

Menus in macOS contain commands for the operating system and any relevant apps. If there is an arrow next to a command it means there are subsequent options for the item. Some menus also incorporate the same transparency as the sidebar so that the background shows through.

...cont'd

Transparency

One feature in macOS Catalina is that the sidebar and toolbars in certain apps are transparent so that you can see some of the Desktop behind it. This also helps the uppermost window blend in with the background:

1 In certain apps with a sidebar, such as the Finder or Safari, the background appears behind the sidebar

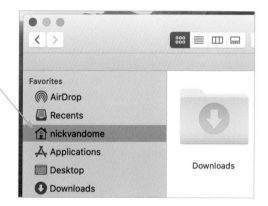

2 When you move the window, the background behind the sidebar changes accordingly

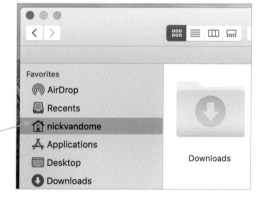

Window buttons

These appear in any open macOS window and can be used to manipulate the window. They include a full-screen option. Use the window buttons to, from left to right: close a window, minimize a window or maximize a window.

If an app has full-screen functionality, this green button is available:

If an option is gray, it means it is not available; i.e. the screen cannot be maximized.

The red window button is used to close a window, and in some cases – such as Notes, Reminders and Calendar – it also closes the app. The amber button is used to minimize a window, so that it appears at the right-hand side of the Dock.

11

About Your Mac

When you buy a new Mac, you will almost certainly check the technical specifications before you make a purchase. Once you have your Mac, there will be times when you will want to view these specifications again, such as the version of macOS in use, the amount of memory and the amount of storage. This can be done through the About This Mac option, which can be accessed from the Apple menu. To do this:

1 Click on the **Apple menu** and click on the **About This Mac** link

2 Click on the **Overview** tab

3 This window contains information about the version of macOS being used; the processor; amount of memory; type of graphics card; and serial number

Hot tip

The System Report section is also where you can check whether your Mac is compatible with the Handoff functionality (covered on page 45), which does not work with most pre-2012 Macs. Click on the **Bluetooth** section in the **System Report** to see if Handoff is supported.

4 Click on the **System Report...** button to view full details about the hardware and software on your Mac

System Report...

5 Click on the **Software Update...** button to see available software updates for your Mac

Display information
This gives information about your Mac's display:

For more information about software updates, see page 181.

1 Click on the **Displays** tab Displays

2 This window contains information about your Mac's display, including the type, size, resolution, and graphics card

3 Click on the **Displays Preferences...** button to view options for changing the display's resolution, brightness and color

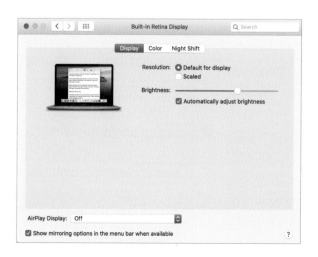

...cont'd

Storage information
This contains information about your Mac's physical and removable storage:

Don't forget

Click on the **Manage...** button in the Storage window to view how much space specific apps are taking up, and also options for optimizing storage on your Mac. With macOS Catalina, this is known as **Optimized Storage**. Optimized Storage includes a **Store in iCloud** option, which can be used to enable your Mac to identify files that have not been opened or used in a long time, and then automatically store them in iCloud (if you have enough storage space there). Their location remains the same on your Mac, but they are physically kept in iCloud, thus freeing up more space on your Mac. Optimized Storage also has options for removing movies and TV shows that have been watched, emptying the Trash automatically and reducing overall clutter on your Mac.

1 Click on the **Storage** tab Storage

2 This window contains information about the used and available storage on your hard disk, and also options for writing various types of CDs and DVDs (if applicable)

Managing memory
This contains information about your Mac's memory, which is used to run macOS and also the applications on your computer:

1 Click on the **Manage...** tab Manage...

2 This window contains information about how memory can be managed in macOS Catalina (see tip)

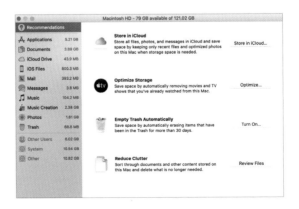

Support

The **Support** tab provides links to a range of help options for your Mac and macOS.

Service

The **Service** tab provides links to service and repair options and also the AppleCare Protection Plan, for extending the initial one-year warranty of your Mac.

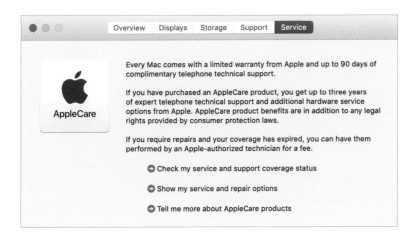

About System Preferences

macOS Catalina has a wide range of options for customizing and configuring the way that your Mac operates. These are located within the System Preferences section. To access this:

Don't forget

For more detailed information about the Dock, see Chapter 2.

Don't forget

For a detailed look at System Preferences, see pages 38-39.

Hot tip

The **General** option in System Preferences can be used to change the overall appearance of macOS Catalina, including colors for buttons, menus, scroll bars and windows. Another option in System Preferences is for **Desktop & Screen Saver**. This has tabs for these items, from which you can select a background wallpaper for your Mac, including the Dynamic Desktop, and also a screen saver for when it is inactive.

1 Click on this button on the Dock (the bar of icons that appears along the bottom of the screen), or access it from the Applications folder

2 All of the options are shown in the **System Preferences** window

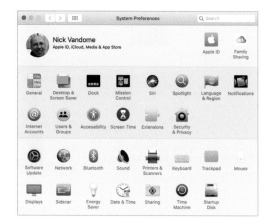

3 Click once on an item to open it in the main System Preferences window. Each item will have a number of options for customization

4 Click on the **Show All** button to return to the main System Preferences window

Search Options

Finding items on a Mac or on the web is an important part of everyday computing, and with macOS Catalina there are a number of options for doing this:

Siri
Siri is Apple's digital voice assistant that can search for items using speech. It has been available on Apple's mobile devices using iOS for a number of years, and with macOS Catalina it is available on Mac desktops and laptops. See pages 18-21 for more details about setting up and using Siri.

Spotlight search
Spotlight is the dedicated search app for macOS. It can be used over all the files on your Mac and the internet. To use Spotlight:

1 Click on this icon at the right of the Apple Menu bar

2 Click in the Spotlight Search box

3 Enter a keyword, or phrase, for which you want to search

4 The top hits from within your apps are shown in the left-hand panel. Click on one to view its details

5 Scroll down the left-hand panel to view different search result options, such as entries from Wikipedia or the web; or a dictionary definition of a word

Finder search
This is the Search box in the top right-hand corner of the Finder and can be used to search for items within it. See page 69 for details about using Finder search.

Using Siri

Siri is the digital voice assistant that can be used to vocally search for a wide range of items from your Mac and the web. Also, the results can be managed in innovative ways so that keeping up-to-date is easier than ever.

Setting up Siri
To set up and start using Siri:

Hot tip

Check **On** the **Show Siri in menu bar** box to show the Siri icon in the top right-hand corner of the main Apple Menu bar.

☑ Show Siri in menu bar

1 Open **System Preferences** and click on the **Siri** button

Siri

2 Check **On** the **Enable Ask Siri** box

3 Make selections here for how Siri operates, including language and the voice used by Siri

Hot tip

An internal or external microphone is required in order to ask Siri questions.

4 Click on the **Siri** icon on the Dock or in the Menu bar to open Siri

5 The Siri window opens, ready for use

What can I help you with?

Searching with Siri

Siri can respond to most requests, including playing a music track, checking the weather, opening photos, and adding calendar events. If you open Siri but do not ask a question, it will prompt you with a list of possible queries. Click on the microphone icon at the bottom of the panel to ask a question. It is also possible to ask questions of Siri while you are working on another document.

Siri can search for a vast range of items, from your Mac or the web. Some useful Siri functions include:

Searching for documents

This can be refined by specifying documents covering a specific date or subject:

1 Ask Siri to find and display documents with certain criteria; e.g. created by a specific person

It is possible to ask Siri to search for specific types of documents; e.g. those created in Pages, or PDF files.

2 Ask Siri to refine the criteria; e.g. only include documents created in a specific app. Click on an item to open it in its related app

...cont'd

Drag and drop results

Once search results have been displayed by Siri they can be managed in a variety of ways. One of these is to copy an item in the search results into another app, by dragging and dropping:

Click on the cross in the top left-hand corner of the Siri window to close it. Otherwise, it can be left open for more queries and searches.

1 Ask Siri to display a certain type of item, such as a map location or an image

2 Drag the resulting item into another app, such as a word processing app or the Notes app

Multitasking

The Siri search window can be left open on the Desktop so that you can ask Siri a question while you are working on something else; e.g. while you are working on a document, ask Siri to display a relevant web page.

Pinning results

Some search results are dynamic; i.e. they change on a regular basis. This includes items such as sports results and weather forecasts. With Siri, these can be pinned to the Notification Center and they will then be updated when they change. To pin Siri search results:

1 Search for a certain item, such as the prices for specific shares on the stock market

2 When Siri returns the result, click on this button to pin the search to the Notification Center

3 The item will be pinned to the Notification Center, which will always display the most recent information, and it will be updated when new details are available

Hot tip

For more information about using the Notification Center, see pages 118-119.

Dark Mode

With macOS Catalina, the background of compatible apps can be turned black in order to make them stand out more. This style may not be for everyone, but it is a useful option if you want to change the appearance of your apps. This is known as Dark Mode:

1 Open **System Preferences**

2 Click on the **General** button

3 Click on the **Dark** button to activate **Dark Mode**

4 The background is turned black, with the text inverted as white. This will apply to all compatible apps, once Dark Mode is activated

5 The dark background can make windows stand out more against items such as the Desktop

Dynamic Desktop

The Desktop background with macOS Catalina can be customized so that it changes appearance depending on the time of day. This is known as the Dynamic Desktop. To use it:

1 Open **System Preferences**

2 Click on the **Desktop & Screen Saver** button

Desktop & Screen Saver

3 Click in the **Catalina** box and select **Dynamic**

4 Click here to select the type of Dynamic Desktop required

5 The appearance of the Dynamic Desktop changes during the day

Don't forget

Click on this icon to set the Dynamic Desktop to an image of the sky, which changes during the day.

Accessibility

In all areas of computing it is important to give as many people access to the system as possible. This includes users with visual impairments and also people who have problems using the mouse and keyboard. In macOS this is achieved through the functions of the Accessibility section of System Preferences. To use these:

Another option in the Accessibility window is for **Switch Control**, which enables a Mac to be controlled by a variety of devices including the mouse, keypad and gamepad devices.

Experiment with the VoiceOver function, if only to see how it operates. This will give you a better idea of how visually-impaired users access information on a computer.

1 Click on the **Accessibility** button in the **System Preferences** folder to display the accessibility options in the left-hand panel

Accessibility

2 Click on the **Display** option to change the settings for display colors and contrast, and to increase the cursor size

3 Click on the **Zoom** option to change the settings for zooming in on the screen

4 Click on the **VoiceOver** option to enable VoiceOver, which provides a spoken description of what is on the screen

5 Click on the **Audio** option to select an on-screen flash for alerts, and settings for how sound is played

The Audio, Keyboard, and Mouse & Trackpad accessibility options have links to additional options within their own System Preferences.

6 Click on the **Keyboard** option to access settings for customizing the keyboard

7 Click on the **Mouse & Trackpad** option to access settings for customizing these devices

8 Click on the **Dictation** option to select preferences for using spoken commands

The Spoken Word

macOS Catalina not only has numerous apps for adding text to documents, emails and messages; it also has a Dictation function so that you can speak what you want to appear on screen. To set up and use the Dictation feature:

1 Click on the **Dictation** tab in **System Preferences** > **Keyboard**

2 By default, the Dictation option is **Off**

3 Click the **On** button to enable Dictation

4 Check On the **Use Enhanced Dictation** button

5 Dictation can be accessed in relevant apps by selecting **Edit** > **Start Dictation** from the Menu bar

6 Start talking when the microphone icon appears. Click **Done** when you have finished recording your text

Hot tip

Punctuation can be added with the Dictation function, by speaking commands such as "comma" or "question mark". These will then be converted into the appropriate symbols.

Don't forget

Dictation settings can also be found in **System Preferences** > **Accessibility** – see Step 8 on page 24.

Shutting Down

The Apple menu (which can be accessed by clicking on the Apple icon at the top-left corner of the Desktop, or any subsequent macOS window) is standardized in macOS. This means that it has the same options regardless of the app in which you are working. This has a number of advantages, not least being the fact that it makes it easier to shut down your Mac. When shutting down, there are three options that can be selected:

- **Sleep**. This puts the Mac into hibernation mode; i.e. the screen goes blank and the hard drive becomes inactive. This state is maintained until the mouse is moved or a key is pressed on the keyboard. This then wakes up the Mac and it is ready to continue work. It is a good idea to add a login password for accessing the Mac when it wakes up, otherwise other people could wake it up and gain access to it. To add a login password, go to **System Preferences** > **Security & Privacy** and click on the **General** tab. Check On the **Require password** checkbox and select from one of the timescale options (**immediately** is best).

- **Restart**. This closes down the Mac and then restarts it again. This can be useful if you have added new software and your computer requires a restart to make it active.

- **Shut Down**. This closes down the Mac completely once you have finished working.

When shutting down, make sure you have saved all of your open documents, although macOS will prompt you to do this if you have forgotten.

If a password is added, the Lock screen will appear whenever the Mac is woken from sleep and the password will be required to unlock it.

Users of the Apple Watch can unlock their Mac running macOS Catalina, without a password.

macOS Catalina has a **Resume** function, where the Mac opens up in the same state as when it was shut down. See page 54 for details.

Click here to access the **Apple menu**

Click here to access one of the shut-down options

2 Getting Up and Running

This chapter looks at some of the essential features of macOS Catalina. These include the Dock for organizing and accessing all of the elements of your Mac computer; the System Preferences for the way your Mac looks and operates; and items for arranging folders and files. It also introduces the online service – iCloud – for sharing digital content, including the Family Sharing feature for sharing your photos, music, apps and books with family members.

Introducing the Dock

The Dock is one of the main organizational elements of macOS. Its main function is to help organize and access apps, folders and files. In addition, with its background and icons, it also makes an aesthetically-pleasing addition to the Desktop. The main things to remember about the Dock are:

- It is divided into two: apps go on the left of the dividing line; all other items, and open apps, go on the right.

- It can be customized in several different ways.

By default, the Dock appears at the bottom of the screen:

Apps go here   Dividing line   Open items

By default, the two icons to the right of the dividing line are:

Downloads. This is for items that you have downloaded from the web. The items can be accessed from here, and opened or run.

Trash. This is where items can be dragged to if you want to remove them. It can also be used to eject removable devices, such as flashdrives, by dragging the device's icon over the Trash. It cannot be removed from the Dock.

28

Apps on the Dock

Opening apps
When you open apps they appear on the Dock and can be worked with within the Dock environment.

1 Click once on an app to open it (either on the Dock, in the Finder Applications folder or the Launchpad). Once an app has been opened, it is displayed on the Dock with a black dot underneath it

Apps can be opened from the Dock, the Finder or the Launchpad. The Finder is covered in detail in Chapter 3, and see pages 98-99 for more on the Launchpad.

2 When windows are opened within the app, they are displayed to the right of the dividing line

3 Click on an icon to the right of the dividing line to maximize it: it disappears from the Dock and displays at full size

4 If a window is minimized by clicking on this button, it goes back to the right-hand side of the dividing line on the Dock

Some apps such as Notes, Reminders and Calendar will close when the active window is closed. Others such as Pages, Keynote and Numbers will remain open even if all of the windows are closed: the recently-accessed documents will be displayed as in the context menu in Step 5.

5 Press and hold underneath an open app to view the available windows for the app (this will differ for individual apps, as some operate by using a single window)

6 To close an open app, press and hold on the black dot underneath its icon on the Dock and click on the **Quit** button (or select its name on the Menu bar and select **Quit**)

Setting Dock Preferences

As with most elements of macOS, the Dock can be modified in numerous ways. This can affect both the appearance of the Dock and the way it operates. To set Dock preferences:

The Dock cannot be moved by dragging it physically; this can only be done in the Dock preferences window.

1 Select **System Preferences** > **Dock**

Dock

2 The Dock preferences allow you to change its size, orientation, the way icons appear with magnification, and effects for when items are minimized

You cannot make the Dock size so large that some of the icons would not be visible on the Desktop. By default, the Dock is resized so that everything is always visible.

3 Drag the Dock **Size** slider to increase or decrease the size of the Dock

The **Position on screen** options enable you to place the Dock on the left, right or bottom of the screen

4 Click on the **Magnification** box and drag the slider to determine the size to which icons are enlarged when the cursor is moved over them

Move the cursor over an icon on the Dock to see the magnification effect.

5 The **Genie effect** under the **Minimize windows using** option shrinks the item to be minimized, like a genie going back into its lamp

Hot tip

Open windows can also be maximized and minimized by double-clicking on the Title bar (the area at the top of the window, next to the three window buttons).

31

Manual resizing

In addition to changing the size of the Dock by using the Dock preferences dialog box, it can also be resized manually:

1 Drag vertically on the Dock dividing line to increase or decrease its size

When the cursor is moved over an item in the Dock, the name of that item is displayed above it.

Move the cursor over a Stack, then press **Ctrl** + **click** to access options for how that Stack is displayed.

Any new items that are added to the folder will also be visible through the Stack.

Using Stacks

Stacks on the Dock

To save space, it is possible to add folders to the Dock, where their contents can easily be accessed. These are known as Stacks. To create Stacks on the Dock:

1 To create a new Stack, drag a folder onto the Dock. Stacked items are placed on the right of the Dock dividing line. Click on a Stack to view its contents

2 Stacks can be viewed as:

- A grid.

- A fan, depending on the number of items it contains.

- A list. Click on a folder to view its contents within a Stack, then click on files to open them in their relevant app.

Stacks on the Desktop

Stacks can also be created on the Desktop, to make it look less cluttered if a lot of files have been placed there. Stacks on the Desktop collate similar file types and create a single Stack for them, which can be expanded as required. To do this:

1 If files are placed on the Desktop they each appear as individual items, which can make the Desktop look untidy

Don't forget

If different file types are placed on the Desktop, they will all be placed into their own relevant Stacks, with a single icon; e.g. document files and image files.

2 Select **View** > **Use Stacks** from the Menu bar to stack all similar file types on the Desktop

3 Similar file types are stacked together with a single icon. Click on the icon to expand the Stack and view the individual files within it

4 Click on this button to contract the Stack back to a single icon

Dock Menus

One of the features of the Dock is that it can display contextual menus for selected items. This means that it shows menus with options that are applicable to the item that is being accessed. This can only be done when an item has been opened.

1 Click and hold on the black dot underneath an item's icon to display the item's individual context menu

Click on **Quit** on the icon's contextual menu to close an open app or file, depending on which side of the dividing bar the item is located.

2 Click on **Show in Finder** to see where the item is located on your computer

Working with Dock Items

Adding items

Numerous items can be added to the Dock; the only restriction is the size of monitor on which to display all of the Dock items. (The size of the Dock can be reduced to accommodate more icons, but you have to be careful that all of the icons are still legible.) To add items to the Dock:

1 Locate the required item in the Finder and drag it onto the Dock. All of the other icons move along to make space for the new one

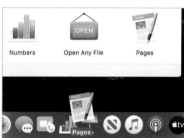

Keep in Dock

Every time you open a new app, its icon will appear in the Dock for the duration that the app is open, even if it has not previously been put in the Dock. If you then decide that you would like to keep it in the Dock, you can enable this as follows:

1 Click and hold on the black dot underneath an open app's icon

2 Select **Options** > **Keep in Dock** to ensure the app remains in the Dock when it is closed

If you are upgrading to macOS Catalina (rather than buying a new Mac), the Dock setup will be the same as the one used with the previous version of the operating system.

Icons on the Dock are shortcuts to the related item, rather than the item itself, which remains in its original location.

You can add numerous items to the Dock, but it will automatically shrink to display all of its items if it becomes too big for the available space.

...cont'd

Removing items

Any item on the left of the dividing line, except the Finder, can be removed from the Dock. However, this does not remove it from your computer; it just removes the shortcut for accessing it. You will still be able to locate it in its folder in the Finder and, if required, drag it back onto the Dock. To remove items from the Dock:

Hot tip

When an icon is dragged from the Dock, it has to be moved a reasonable distance before the **Remove** alert appears.

 1 Drag the item away from the Dock until it displays the **Remove** tag. The item disappears once the cursor is released. All of the other icons then move up to fill in the space

Removing open apps

You can remove an app from the Dock, even if it is open and running. To do this:

1 Drag an app off the Dock while it is running. Initially, the icon will remain on the Dock because the app is still open

Don't forget

If **Keep in Dock** has been selected for an item (see page 35) the app will remain in the Dock even when it has been closed.

2 When the app is closed (click and hold on the dot underneath the item and select **Quit**) its icon will be removed from the Dock

Trash

The Trash folder is a location for placing items that you do not need anymore. However, when items are placed in the Trash, they are not removed from your computer. This requires another command, as the Trash is really a holding area before you decide you want to remove items permanently. The Trash can also be used for ejecting removable disks attached to your Mac.

Sending items to the Trash
Items can be sent to the Trash by dragging them from the location in which they are stored.

1 Drag an item over the **Trash** icon to place it in the Trash folder

2 Click once on the **Trash** icon on the Dock to view its contents

Items can also be sent to the Trash by selecting them in the Finder and then selecting **File** > **Move to Trash** from the Menu bar.

All of the items within the Trash can be removed in a single command: select **Finder** > **Empty Trash** from the Menu bar to remove all of the items in the Trash folder.

System Preferences

In macOS there are preferences that can be set for just about every aspect of your computer. This gives you greater control over how the interface looks and how the operating system functions. To access System Preferences:

1 Click on this icon on the Dock or from the Applications folder in the Finder

macOS Catalina supports multiple displays, which means you can connect your Mac to two or more displays and view different content on each one. The Dock appears on the active screen, and each screen also has its own Menu bar. Different full-screen apps can also be viewed on each screen.

Apple ID. This contains options for setting up an Apple ID for use with iCloud, the online sharing and storage service.

Family Sharing. This can be used to set up and use Family Sharing, for sharing music, movies, games, apps and books with up to five other family members.

General. Options for the overall look of buttons, menus, windows and scroll bars.

Desktop & Screen Saver. This can be used to change the Desktop background and the screen saver.

Dock. Options for the way the Dock looks and functions.

Mission Control. This gives you a variety of options for managing all of your open windows and apps.

Siri. This can be used to turn on or off the digital voice assistant, Siri, and also set voice style and language.

Spotlight. This can be used to specify settings for the macOS search facility, Spotlight.

Language & Region. Options for the language used on your Mac.

Notifications. This can be used to set up how you are notified about items such as email, messages and software updates.

The **Internet Accounts** section can be used to set up email accounts and also link to your social networking accounts such as Facebook, Twitter and LinkedIn.

Internet Accounts. This can be used to link to other online accounts that you have (see Hot tip).

Users & Groups. This can be used to create accounts for different users on your Mac.

Accessibility. This can be used to set options for users who have difficulty with viewing text on screen, hearing commands, using the keyboard or using the mouse.

Screen Time. This can be used to show screen usage and limit access to the computer and various online functions.

Extensions. This can be used to customize your Mac with extensions and plug-ins from Apple and third-party developers.

Security & Privacy. This enables you to secure your Home folder with a master password, for added security.

Software Update. This can be used to specify how software updates are handled. It connects to the App Store to access the available updates.

Network. This can be used to specify network settings for connecting to the internet or other computers.

Bluetooth. Options for attaching Bluetooth wireless devices.

Sound. Options for adding sound effects, and playing and recording sound.

Printers & Scanners. Options for selecting printers and scanners.

Keyboard. Options for how the keyboard functions; your keyboard shortcuts; and dictation settings.

Trackpad. Options for when you are using a trackpad.

Mouse. Options for how the mouse functions.

Displays. Options for the screen display, such as resolution.

Sidecar. This can be used to connect to an iPad, to use it as an additional monitor for a Mac.

Energy Saver. Options for when the computer is inactive.

Date & Time. Options for changing the computer's date and time to time zones around the world.

Sharing. This can be used to specify how files are shared over a network. This is also covered on page 169.

Time Machine. This can be used to configure and set up the macOS backup facility.

Startup Disk. This can be used to specify the disk from which your computer starts up. This is usually the macOS volume.

Apple ID, Family Sharing, Screen Time and Sidecar are all new individual System Preferences in macOS Catalina.

About iCloud

Cloud computing is an attractive proposition and one that has gained great popularity in recent years. As a concept, it consists of storing your content on an external computer server. This not only gives you added security in terms of backing up your information; it also means that the content can then be shared over a variety of devices.

iCloud is Apple's consumer Cloud computing product that consists of online services such as email; a calendar; notes; contacts; and saving photos and documents. iCloud provides users with a way to save and back up their files and content to the online service, and then use them across their Apple devices such as other Mac computers, iPhones, iPads and iPod Touches.

About iCloud

Once iCloud has been set up (see next page) it can be accessed from within System Preferences:

1 Click on the **Apple ID** button

2 Click on the **iCloud** button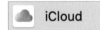

You can use iCloud to save and share the following between your different devices, with an Apple ID account (see next page):

- Photos
- Mail and Safari
- Documents
- Backups
- Notes
- Reminders
- Contacts and Calendar

When you save an item to iCloud it automatically pushes it to all of your other compatible devices; you do not have to manually sync anything as iCloud does it all for you.

The standard iCloud service is free, and this includes an iCloud email address and 5GB of online storage. (*Correct at the time of printing.*)

Accessing iCloud from the Apple ID button in System Preferences is a new feature in macOS Catalina.

There is also a version of iCloud for Windows, which can be accessed for download from the Apple website at **https://support.apple. com/en-us/HT204283**

Setting up iCloud

To use iCloud with macOS Catalina you need to first have an Apple ID. This is a service you can register for to be able to access a range of Apple facilities, including iCloud. You can register with an email address and a password. When you first start using iCloud you will be prompted for your Apple ID details. If you do not have an Apple ID you can create one at this point.

1 Open System Preferences and click on the **Sign In** button next to **Sign in to your Apple ID**

2 Sign in with your Apple ID, or

3 Click on the **Create Apple ID...** link and follow the steps to create your Apple ID

4 Open System Preferences and click on the **iCloud** button

5 Check on the items you want included within iCloud. All of these items will be backed up and shared across all of your Apple devices

When you have an Apple ID and an iCloud account, you can also use the iCloud website to access your content. Access the website at **www.icloud.com** and log in with your Apple ID details.

The online iCloud service includes your online email service; Contacts; Calendars; Reminders; Notes; and versions of Pages, Keynote and Numbers. You can log in to your iCloud account from any internet-enabled device.

About the iCloud Drive

One of the options in the iCloud section is for the iCloud Drive. This can be used to store documents and other content so that you can use them on any other Apple devices that you have, such as an iPhone or an iPad. With the iCloud Drive you can start work on a document on one device, and continue on another device from where you left off. To set up the iCloud Drive:

1 Click on the **Apple ID** > **iCloud** button in System Preferences, as shown on page 40

2 Check **On** the **iCloud Drive** option and click on the **Options...** button

3 Select the items to use with the iCloud Drive. In macOS Catalina, this includes the **Desktop & Documents Folders** option, which ensures that any items saved into these locations will be stored in the iCloud Drive

Beware

If the **Desktop & Documents Folders** option is selected for the iCloud Drive this can take up a lot of iCloud storage, as all items in these locations will be saved to the iCloud Drive, which counts towards your iCloud storage limit.

4 Click on the **Done** button

42

Using the iCloud Drive
To work with files in the iCloud Drive:

1 In the Finder sidebar click on the **iCloud Drive** button

2 Certain iCloud Drive folders are already created, based on the apps that you have selected on the previous page. These are the default folders into which content from their respective apps will be placed (although others can also be selected, if required). Double-click on a folder to view its contents

3 To save files into an iCloud Drive folder, select **File > Save As** from the Menu bar, click on the **iCloud Drive** button in the Finder sidebar, and navigate to the required folder for the file

Pages is the Apple app for word processing; Numbers for spreadsheets; and Keynote for presentations. These can all be downloaded from the App Store, if they do not come pre-installed on your Mac.

43

Another useful iCloud function is the iCloud Keychain (**System Preferences > iCloud** and check on the **Keychain** option). If this is enabled, it can keep all of your passwords and credit card information up-to-date across multiple devices and remember them when you use them on websites. The information is encrypted and controlled through your Apple ID.

Hot tip

It is also possible to continue an email with the Continuity feature. First, create it on your Mac and then close it. You will be prompted to save the email as a draft and if you do this, you will be able to open it from the **Drafts** mailbox on another Apple device.

Macs running macOS Catalina and a compatible iPad can also be linked using the **Sidecar** option in **System Preferences**. This enables the iPad to be used as an additional monitor for the Mac. This is a new feature in macOS Catalina. Click on the **Sidecar** button and select the required device under the **Connect to** heading.

Continuity

One of the themes of macOS Catalina and iOS for mobile devices (iOS 8 and later) is to make all of your content available on all of your Apple devices. This is known as Continuity: when you create something on one device you can then pick it up and finish it on another. This is done through iCloud. To do this:

1 Ensure the app has iCloud activated, as on page 41

2 Create the content in an app on your Mac

3 Open the same app on another Apple device; e.g. an iPad. The item created on your Mac should be available to view and edit. Any changes will then show up on the file on your Mac, too

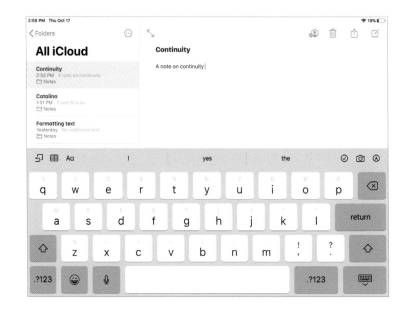

Handoff

Handoff is one of the key features of Continuity and it displays icons of items that you have opened on other devices, such as Safari web pages. Handoff does not work with all devices; it only works if both devices have OS X Yosemite or later, and iOS 8 or later, for mobile devices.

To use Handoff you will need to do the following:

- Your Mac must be running OS X Yosemite (or later) and your mobile device (iPhone 5 and later; iPad Pro; iPad 4 and later; all models of iPad mini; and the 5th-generation iPod Touch) must have iOS 8 (or later).

- Your Mac has to support Bluetooth 4.0, which means that most pre-2012 Macs are not compatible with Handoff.

To check if your Mac supports Handoff:

The apps that work with Handoff include Mail, Safari, Maps, Messages, Reminders, Calendar, Contacts, Notes, Pages, Numbers and Keynote.

1 Select **Apple Menu** > **About This Mac** > **System Report**.
Click on **Bluetooth** to see if Handoff is supported

Bluetooth Low Energy Supported:	Yes
Handoff Supported:	Yes
Instant Hot Spot Supported:	Yes

2 Turn on Bluetooth on your Mac (via System Preferences) and on your mobile device (via Settings)

3 Turn on Handoff on your Mac (**System Preferences** > **General** and check on **Allow Handoff Between this Mac and your iCloud Devices**) and on your mobile device (**Settings** > **General** > **Handoff**)

If Handoff is not working, try turning both devices off and on and do the same with Bluetooth. Also, try logging out, and then back in, to your iCloud account on both devices.

4 When Handoff is activated, compatible apps will be displayed at the left-hand side of the Dock when they have been opened on another device

Safari
From iPhone

About Family Sharing

As everyone gets more and more digital devices it is becoming increasingly important to be able to share content with other people, particularly family members. In macOS Catalina, and iCloud, the Family Sharing function enables you to share items that you have downloaded from the relevant online Apple store with your Apple ID, such as music and movies, with up to five other family members, as long as they have an Apple ID. To set up Family Sharing:

To use Family Sharing, other family members must have an Apple device using either iOS 8 (or later) for a mobile device (iPad, iPhone or iPod Touch) or OS X Yosemite (or later) for a desktop or laptop Mac computer.

1 Once you have signed in to your Apple ID, click on the **Family Sharing** button in System Preferences

Family Sharing

2 Click on the **Next** button

3 If you are the Organizer of Family Sharing, i.e. the one who manages it, click on the **Next** button

4 If you want to share your Apple ID purchases, check **On** the **Share your purchases** button and click on the **Next** button

5 Click on the **Next** button to confirm your payment method for your Apple ID

6 Click on the **Agree** button to accept the Family Sharing terms and conditions

7 Check **On the Share your location** option so that family members can locate your devices. Click on the **Done** button

8 Click on the **Add Family Member...** button to send an invitation to someone you want to join Family Sharing. They have to accept this before they can participate in Family Sharing

A Family Sharing invitation can be sent by email or using the Messages app.

Using Family Sharing

Once Family Sharing has been set up it can be used by members of the group to share music, apps, movies and books. There is also a shared Family calendar that can be used, and it is also possible to view the location of the devices of the family members.

Sharing music
To share music and other content from the Music app:

1 Click on the **Music** app on the Dock

2 Click on the **iTunes Store** button in the left-hand sidebar

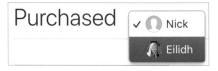

MUSIC QUICK LINKS

Redeem   Account
Send Gift   Support

Beats 1
iTunes Match

Purchased

3 Click on the **Purchased** link

4 By default, your own purchases are displayed. Click on the drop-down option next to the **Purchased** link to view other members of Family Sharing

5 Click on another family member to view their purchases (they will be able to do this for your purchases, too)

6 Click on the iCloud button to download the other family member's music tracks or albums to your device

Hot tip

You have to be connected to the internet and be online to access the Music app's iTunes Store and view purchases from other family members. When you do this, you can play their songs without having to download them. However, if you want to be able to use them when you are offline then you will have to download them first, as in Step 5.

Sharing apps

Apps can also be shared from the App Store. To do this:

1 Click on the **App Store** app on the Dock

2 Click on the account name button

3 By default, your own purchases are displayed. Click on the drop-down option to view other members of Family Sharing

4 Click on another family member to view and then download their purchased apps (they will be able to do this for your apps, too)

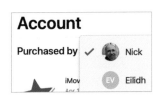

Sharing books

Books can also be shared in a similar way to items from the Music app and the App Store. To do this:

1 Click on the **Books** app on the Dock

2 Click on the **Book Store** button

3 Click on the **Purchased** link, under the **Quick Links** heading

4 By default, your own purchases are displayed. Click on the **Purchased** account drop-down option

to view other members of Family Sharing and any books they have downloaded

More than one family member can use content in the Family Sharing group at the same time.

...cont'd

Sharing calendars

Family Sharing also generates a Family calendar that can be used by all Family Sharing members:

Don't forget

Other members of the Family Sharing group can add items to the Family calendar and when they do, you will be sent a notification that appears on your Mac.

Hot tip

To change the color of a calendar, click on the **Calendars** button at the top left of the window. **Ctrl + click** on a calendar name and select a color from the bottom of the panel, or click on **Custom Color...** to choose from the full spectrum.

1 Open the **Calendar** app

2 Double-click on a date to create a **New Event**. The current calendar (shown in the top right-hand corner) will probably not be the Family one. Click on this button to change the calendar

3 Click on the **Family** calendar

4 Complete the details for the event. It will be added to your calendar, with the Family color tag. Other people in your Family Sharing circle will have this event added to their Family calendar, and they will also be sent a notification

Finding lost family devices

Family Sharing also makes it possible to see where everyone's devices are, which can be useful for locating people, but particularly so if a device belonging to a Family Sharing member is lost or stolen. To do this:

1 Ensure that the **Find My Mac** function is turned on in the **iCloud** System Preferences, and log in to your online iCloud account at **www.icloud.com**

2 Click on the **Find iPhone** button (this works for other Apple devices, too)

3 Devices that are turned on, online and with iCloud activated are shown by green dots

4 Click on a green dot to display information about the device. Click on the **i** symbol to access options for managing the device remotely

5 There are options to send an alert sound to the device, lock it remotely or erase its contents (if you are concerned about it having fallen into the wrong hands)

Lost or missing Apple devices can be searched for from a Mac, using the **Find My** app. The missing devices have to be linked to the same Apple ID or be connected via Family Sharing. This is a new feature in macOS Catalina.

The location of devices is shown on a map, and you can zoom in on the map to see their location more accurately.

51

Desktop Items

If required, the Desktop can be used to store apps and files. However, the Finder (see Chapter 3) does such a good job of organizing all of the elements within your computer that the Desktop is rendered largely redundant, unless you feel happier storing items here. The Desktop can also display any removable disks that are connected to your computer:

Hot tip

Icons for removable disks (e.g. flashdrives) will only become visible on the Desktop once a disk has been inserted.

If a removable disk is connected to your computer, double-click the Desktop icon to view its contents

Don't forget

Any removable disks that are connected to your computer can also be viewed by clicking on them in the sidebar in the Finder.

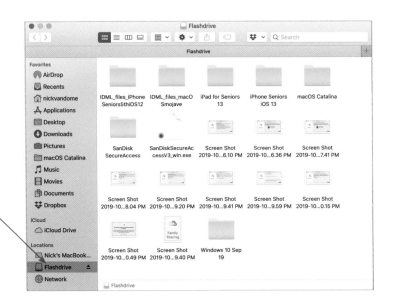

Ejecting Items

If you have removable disks attached to your Mac it is essential to be able to eject them quickly and easily. In macOS there are two ways in which this can be done:

 In the Finder, click on this icon to the right of the name of the removable disk, or

② On the Desktop, click and drag the disk icon over the **Trash**. This turns the Trash icon into the **Eject** icon, and the disk will be ejected

Hot tip

If the Desktop items are not showing, open the Finder and click on **Finder** > **Preferences...** on the Menu bar and click on the **General** tab. Under **Show these items on the desktop** check on the items you want, including **Hard Disks**, **External Disks** and **CDs, DVDs, and iPods**.

③ Some disks, such as CDs and DVDs (if they are connected with an external SuperDrive), are physically ejected when either of these two actions are performed. Other disks, such as flashdrives, have to be removed manually once they have been ejected by macOS. If the disk is not ejected first, the following warning message will appear:

Resuming

One of the chores about computing is that when you close down your computer, you have to first close down all of your open documents and apps and then open them all again when you turn your machine back on. However, macOS Catalina has a feature that allows you to continue working exactly where you left off, even if you turn off your computer. To do this:

1 Before you close down, all of your open documents and apps are available (as shown)

Beware

If you have open, unsaved documents you will be prompted to save them before your Mac is closed down.

2 Select the **Shut Down...** or **Restart...** option from the **Apple menu**

3 Make sure this box is checked **On** (this will ensure that all of your items will appear as before, after the Mac is closed down and then started up again)

☑ Reopen windows when logging back in

4 Confirm the **Shut Down** or **Restart** command

3 Finder

The principal method for moving around macOS Catalina is the Finder. This enables you to access items and organize your apps, folders and files. This chapter looks at how to use the Finder and how to get the most out of this powerful tool, which is at the heart of navigating around macOS. It covers accessing items, how to customize the interface, and options for working with folders.

Working with the Finder

If you were only able to use one item on the Dock it would be the Finder. This is the gateway to all of the elements of your Mac. While it is possible to get to selected items through other routes, the Finder is the only location where you can gain access to everything on your system. If you ever feel that you are getting lost within macOS, click on the Finder and then you should begin to feel more at home. To access the Finder:

 Click once on this icon on the Dock

Overview

The Finder has its own toolbar; a sidebar from which items can be accessed; and a main window, where the contents of selected items can be viewed:

A link to the iCloud Drive is also included in the Finder sidebar.

The Actions button has options for displaying information about a selected item and also options for how it is displayed within the Finder (see page 74 for details).

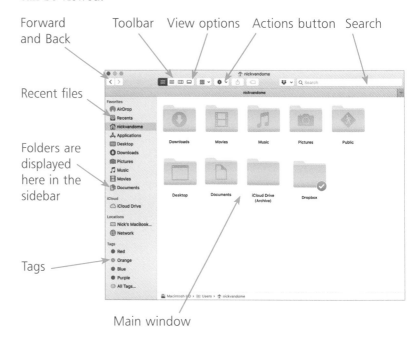

Forward and Back · Toolbar · View options · Actions button · Search

Recent files

Folders are displayed here in the sidebar

Tags

Main window

Finder Folders

Recents

This contains all of the latest files in which you have been working. They are sorted into categories according to file type so that you can search through them quickly. This is an excellent way to locate items without having to look through a lot of folders. To access this:

1 Click on this link in the Finder sidebar to access the contents of your **Recents** folder

2 All of your files are displayed in individual categories. Click on the headings at the top of each category to sort items by those criteria

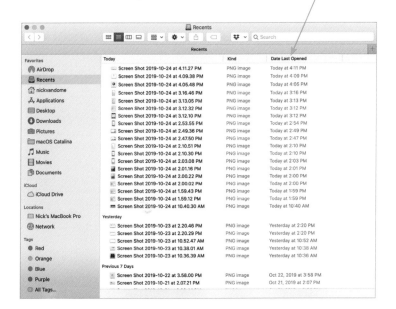

3 Double-click an item to open it from the Finder

The Finder is always open (as denoted by the black dot underneath its icon on the Dock) and it cannot readily be closed down or removed.

The Finder sidebar has the macOS Catalina transparency feature, so that you can see some of the open window, or Desktop, behind it.

57

To change the display of folders in the sidebar, click on the **Finder** menu on the top toolbar. Select **Preferences...** and click on the **Sidebar** tab. Under **Show these items in the sidebar** select the items you want included.

...cont'd

Home folder

This contains the contents of your own Home directory, containing your personal folders and files. macOS inserts some pre-named folders that it thinks will be useful, but it is possible to rearrange or delete these as you please. It is also possible to add as many more folders as you want.

 Applications

This folder contains all of the applications on your Mac. They can also be accessed from the Launchpad, as shown on pages 98-99.

Documents

This is part of your Home folder but is put on the Finder sidebar for ease of access. New folders can be created for different types of documents.

1 Click on your Apple ID account name in the sidebar to access the contents of your **Home** folder

 nickvandome

2 The Home folder contains the **Public** folder, which can be used to share files with other users if the computer is part of a network

When you are creating documents, macOS by default recognizes their type, and then when you save them, suggests the most applicable folder in which to save them.

3 To add a new folder, click the **Actions** button (see page 74), then **New Folder** (or **Ctrl + click** in the window and select **New Folder**). The new folder will open in the main window, named "untitled folder". Overtype the name with one of your choice

4 To delete a folder from the Finder sidebar, **Ctrl + click** on it and select **Remove from Sidebar**

Finder Views

The way in which items are displayed within the Finder can be amended in a variety of ways, depending on how you want to view the contents of a folder. Different folders can have their own viewing options applied to them, and these will stay in place until a new option is specified.

Back button

When working within the Finder, each new window replaces the previous one, unless you open a new app. This prevents the screen becoming cluttered with dozens of open windows, as you look through various Finder windows for a particular item. To ensure that you never feel lost within the Finder structure, there is a Back button on the Finder toolbar that enables you to retrace the steps that you have taken.

1 Navigate to a folder within the Finder (in this example, the **macOS Catalina** folder contained within **Pictures**)

Select an item within the Finder window and click on the space bar to view its details.

59

2 Click on the **Back** button to move back to the previously-visited window (in this example, the main **Pictures** window)

If you have not opened any Finder windows, the Back button will not operate.

< >

...cont'd

Icon view

One of the viewing options for displaying items within the Finder is as icons. This provides a pictorial representation of the items in the Finder. It is possible to customize the way that Icon view looks and functions.

1 Click here on the Finder toolbar to access **Icon** view

2 Select **View** from the Menu bar, check On **as Icons** and select **Show View Options** to access the options for customizing Icon view

3 Drag this slider to set the icon size

4 Select an option for the way icons are arranged in Finder windows

5 Select an option for the background of the Finder window

...cont'd

List view

List view can be used to show the items within a Finder window as a list, with additional information shown next to them. This can be a more efficient method than Icon view if there are a lot of items within a folder, as List view enables you to see more items at one time and also view the additional information.

1 Click here on the Finder toolbar to access **List** view

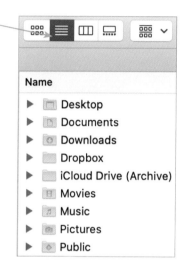

2 The name of each folder or file is displayed here. If folders below the top-level folders have additional items within them, this is denoted by a small triangle next to them. Additional information in List view, such as file size and last modified date, is included in columns to the right

Column view

Column view is a useful option if you want to trace the location of a particular item (i.e. see the full path of its location) starting from the hard drive:

1 Click here on the Finder toolbar to access **Column** view

2 Click on an item to see everything within that folder. If an arrow follows an item, it means that there are further items to view

Gallery View

Another of the view options on the Finder toolbar is the Gallery view: this is a view that has considerable functionality in terms of viewing details of specific files and also applying some quick editing functions to them without having to open the files. To use the Gallery view:

1 Select a file in either Icon, List or Column view and click on this button on the Finder toolbar

2 The item is displayed in the main window, with thumbnails of the other available files below it

3 The item that is displayed will change depending on the type of file that is selected

Quick Look

Through a Finder option called Quick Look, it is possible to view the content of a file without having to first open it. To do this:

1 Select a file in any of the Finder views

2 Press the space bar

3 The contents of the file are displayed without it opening in its default program. Click on the **Markup** button on the top toolbar to add Markup items, such as drawing or writing

4 Click on the cross to close Quick Look, or view the item in full screen

Finder Toolbar

Customizing the toolbar

As with most elements of macOS, it is possible to customize the Finder toolbar. To do this:

Beware

Do not put too many items on the Finder toolbar as you may not be able to see them all in the Finder window. If there are additional toolbar items, there will be a directional arrow indicating this. Click on the arrow to view the available items.

1 Select **View** > **Customize Toolbar...** from the Menu bar

2 Drag individual items from the window into the toolbar

3 Alternatively, drag the default set of icons into the toolbar

4 Click **Done** at the bottom of the window

Finder Sidebar

Using the sidebar

The sidebar is the left-hand panel of the Finder that can be used to access items on your Mac. To use this:

1 Click on a button on the sidebar

2 Its contents are displayed in the main Finder window

Adding to the sidebar

Items that you access most frequently can be added to the sidebar.

1 Drag an item from the main Finder window onto the sidebar

2 A blue line appears determining the location, and the item is added to the sidebar at this point. You can do this with apps, folders and files

When you click on an item in the sidebar, its contents are shown in the main Finder window to the right.

When items are added to the Finder sidebar, a shortcut – or alias – is inserted into the sidebar, not the actual item.

Items can be removed from the sidebar by **Ctrl + clicking** on them and selecting **Remove from Sidebar** from the contextual menu.

Working with Folders

Folders are always denoted by a folder icon. In Icon view they are larger than in List or Column views.

You can create as many "nested" folders (i.e. folders within other folders) as you want, although this can make your folder structure more complicated. Folders can also be dragged over other folders, and if you pause before you release the first folder you will be able to view the content of the target folder, to make sure this is where you want to place the first folder. This is known as spring-loaded folders.

Content can be added to an empty folder by dragging it from another folder and dropping it into the new one.

When macOS Catalina is installed, there are various folders that have already been created to hold apps and files. Some of these are essential (i.e. those containing apps), while others are created as an aid for where you might want to store the files that you create (such as the Pictures and Movies folders). Once you start working with macOS Catalina, you will probably want to create your own folders in which to store and organize your documents. This can be done on the Desktop or within any level of your existing folder structure. To create a new folder:

1 Access the location in which you want to create the new folder (e.g. your Home folder) and select **File > New Folder** from the Menu bar

2 A new, empty folder is inserted at the selected location (named "untitled folder")

3 Overtype the file name with a new one. Press **Enter**

4 Double-click on the folder to view its contents (at this point it should be empty)

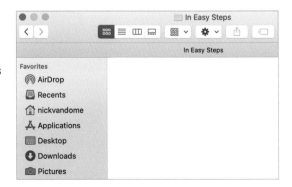

Selecting Items

Apps and files within macOS folders can be selected by a variety of different methods.

Selecting by dragging

Click and drag the cursor to encompass the items to be selected. The selected items will become highlighted.

Once items have been selected, a single command can be applied to all of them. For instance, you can copy a group of items by selecting them and then applying the **Copy** command from the Menu bar.

Selecting by clicking

Click once on an item to select it, hold down Shift, and then click on another item in a list to select a consecutive group of items.

To select a non-consecutive group, select the first item by clicking on it once, then hold down the Command key (**cmd ⌘**) and select the other required items. The selected items will appear highlighted.

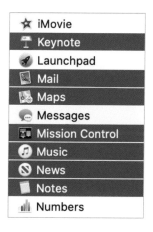

To select all of the items in a folder, select **Edit** > **Select All** from the Menu bar. The Select All command selects all of the elements within the active item. For instance, if the active item is a word processing document, the Select All command will select all of the items within the document; if it is a folder, it will select all of the items within that folder. You can also click **cmd** + **A** to select all items.

Copying and Moving Items

Items can be copied and moved within macOS by using the copy and paste method, or by dragging.

Don't forget

When an item is copied, it is placed on the Clipboard and remains there until another item is copied.

Copy and paste

1 Select an item (or items) and select **Edit > Copy** from the Menu bar

Hot tip

macOS Catalina supports the Universal Clipboard, where items can be copied on a device such as an iPhone and then pasted directly into a document on a Mac running macOS Catalina. The mobile device has to be running iOS 10 (or later) and the Mac has to support the Universal Clipboard. The process is the same as regular copy and paste, except that each operation is performed on the separate device and each app used has to be set up for iCloud. Also, Bluetooth and Wi-Fi have to be activated on both devices.

2 Move to the target location and select **Edit > Paste Item(s)** from the Menu bar. The item is then pasted into the new location

3 To view the items that have been copied onto the clipboard select **Edit > Show Clipboard** from the Menu bar. The items are displayed in the Clipboard window

Clipboard
116.JPG
118.JPG
117.JPG

Dragging

Drag a file from one location to another to move it to that location. (This requires two or more Finder windows to be open, or drag the item over a folder on the sidebar.)

Finder Search

Searching electronic data is now a massive industry, with companies such as Google leading the way with online searching. On Macs it is also possible to search your folders and files, using the built-in search facilities: the Finder search; Siri (see pages 18-21); or Spotlight search (see page 17).

Using Finder
To search for items within the Finder:

1 In the Finder window, enter the search keyword(s) in this box. Search options are listed below the keyword

2 Select an option for which category you want to search over

3 The search results are shown in the Finder window. Click on one of these buttons to search specific areas

4 Double-click on an item to open it

Try to make your search keywords and phrases as accurate as possible. This will create a better list of search results.

Both folders and files will be displayed in the Finder as part of the search results.

Finder Tabs

Tabs in web browsers are now well established, and allow you to have several pages open within the same browser window. This technology is included in the Finder in macOS Catalina, with Finder Tabs. This enables different folders to be open in different tabs within the Finder, so that you can organize your content exactly how you want. To do this:

In macOS Catalina, tabs are available in a range of apps that open multiple windows, including the Apple productivity apps: Pages, Numbers and Keynote. If the tabs are not showing, select **View** > **Show Tab Bar** from the app's Menu bar.

1 Select **View** > **Show Tab Bar** from the Finder menu

2 A new tab appears at the right-hand side of the Finder

3 Click on this button to open the new tab

4 At this point, the content in the new tab is displayed in the window (see the second Hot tip)

To specify an option for what appears in the default window for a new Finder window tab, click on the **Finder** menu and click on **Preferences**, then the **General** tab. Under **New Finder windows show**, select the default window to be used.

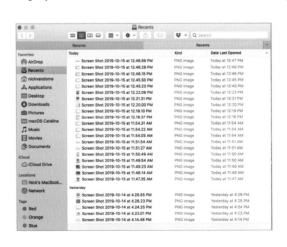

70

5   Access a new folder to display this as the content for the tab. In this way, you can use different tabs for different types of content such as photos or music, or for different topics such as Work, Travel or Finance within Documents

Beware

Dozens of tabs can be added in the Finder. However, when there are too many to fit along the Tab bar they are stacked on top of each other, so it can be hard to work out what you have in your tabs.

71

6   Each tab view can be customized, and this is independent of the other tabs

Tagging in the Finder

When creating content in macOS Catalina, you may find that you have documents of different types that cover the same topic. For instance, you may have work-related documents in Pages for reports, Keynote for presentations, and Numbers for spreadsheets. With the Finder Tags function it is possible to link items with related content through the use of colored tags. These can be added to items in the Finder and also in apps when content is created.

Hot tip

Tags can also be added to items by **Ctrl + clicking** on them and selecting the required tag from the context menu that appears. Also, they can be added from this button on the main Finder toolbar.

1 The tags are listed in the Finder sidebar. (If you can't see the list, hover the cursor over the Tags heading and then click the **Show** button)

2 To give tags specific names, **Ctrl + click** on one, and click on the **Rename** option

Hot tip

Tags can be dragged onto the Dock so that all items with a specific tag can be accessed from here. To do this, drag the tag from the Finder sidebar to the right-hand side of the Dock's dividing line. This will create a Stack containing all of the items with the selected tag.

3 To add tags, select the required items in the Finder window

4 Drag the selected items over the appropriate tag

5 The tags are added to the selected items

Adding tags in apps

Tags can also be added when documents are created in certain apps, such as Pages, Keynote and Numbers.

1 Select **File > Save** (or **Save As**), click in the **Tags** box and select the required tag. Click on the **Save** button

Tags can also be added to iCloud documents so that when you are viewing content in iCloud, all tagged items can be viewed together.

Viewing tags

To view all documents that have had the same tag added:

1 Click on the required tag in the Finder sidebar. All of the tagged documents will be displayed, regardless of their content type or where they are saved on your Mac

Actions Button

The Finder Actions button provides a variety of options for any item, or items, selected in the Finder. To use this:

1 Select an item, or group of items, about which you want to find out additional information

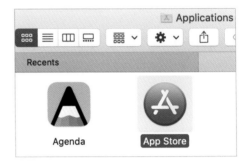

2 Click on the **Actions** button on the Finder toolbar

3 The available options for the selected item, or items, are displayed. These include **Get Info**, which displays additional information about an item such as file type, file size, creation and modification dates, and the default app for opening the item(s)

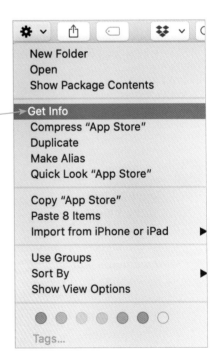

Sharing from the Finder

Also on the Finder toolbar is the Share button. This can be used to share a selected item, or items, in a variety of ways appropriate to the type of file that has been selected. For instance, a photo will have options including the photo-sharing site Flickr, while a text document will have fewer options. To share items directly from the Finder:

1 Locate and select the item(s) that you want to share

This button on the Finder is for changing the arrangement of items within the Finder. Click on this to access arrangement options such as Name, Date and Size.

2 Click on the **Share** button on the Finder toolbar and select one of the options

3 For some of the options, such as Twitter and Flickr, you will be asked to add an account. If you already have an account with these services you can enter the details; or, if not, you can create a new account

You can also add your social networking accounts from **System Preferences > Internet Accounts**. Select the required account and enter your login details.

Menus

The main Apple Menu bar in macOS Catalina contains a variety of menus, which are accessed when the Finder is the active window. When individual apps are open they have their own Menu bars, although in a lot of cases these are similar to the standard Menu bar, particularly for the built-in macOS Catalina apps such as Calendar, Contacts and Notes.

- **Apple menu**. This is denoted by a translucent blue apple and contains general information about the computer, links to the System Preferences and the App Store for app updates, and options for closing down your Mac.

- **Finder menu**. This contains preference options for amending the functionality and appearance of the Finder, and also options for emptying the Trash and accessing other apps (under the Services option).

- **File menu**. This contains common commands for working with open documents, such as opening and closing files, creating aliases, moving to the Trash, ejecting external devices and burning discs.

- **Edit menu**. This contains common commands that apply to the majority of apps used on the Mac. These include Undo, Cut, Copy, Paste, Select All and Show the contents of the Clipboard; i.e. items that have been cut or copied.

- **View menu**. This contains options for how windows and folders are displayed within the Finder, and for customizing the Finder toolbar. This includes showing or hiding the Finder sidebar and selecting view options for the size at which icons are displayed within Finder windows.

- **Go menu**. This can be used to navigate around your computer. This includes moving to your Recents folder, your Home folder, your Applications folder and recently-accessed folders.

- **Window menu**. This contains commands to organize the currently-open apps and files on your Desktop.

- **Help menu**. This contains the Mac Help files, which contain information about all aspects of macOS Catalina.

4 Navigating in macOS Catalina

macOS Catalina has

Multi-Touch Gestures for

navigating around your apps

and documents. This chapter

looks at how to use these to get

around your Mac and also at

using Mission Control.

The macOS Way of Navigating

One of the most revolutionary features of earlier versions of OS X, which is continued with macOS Catalina, is the way in which you can navigate around your applications, web pages and documents. This involves a much greater reliance on swiping on a trackpad or adapted mouse; techniques that have been imported from the iPhone and the iPad. These are known as Multi-Touch Gestures, and to take full advantage of these you will need to have one of the following devices:

- **A trackpad**. This can be found on MacBooks.

- **A Magic Trackpad**. This can be used with an iMac, a Mac mini or a Mac Pro. It works wirelessly via Bluetooth.

- **A Magic Mouse**. This can be used with an iMac, a Mac mini or a Mac Pro. It works wirelessly via Bluetooth.

All of these devices work using a swiping technique with fingers moving over their surface. This should be done with a light touch; it is a gentle swipe, rather than any pressure being applied to the device.

The trackpads and Magic Mouse do not have any buttons in the same way as traditional devices. Instead, specific areas are clickable so that you can still perform left- and right-click operations.

On a Magic Mouse, the center and right side can be used for clicking operations, and on a Magic Trackpad, the left and right corners can perform the same tasks.

Models of MacBooks from May 2015 onwards (and the Magic Trackpad 2) employ a technology known as Force Touch. This provides the user with different options, depending on how firmly they press on the trackpad. This means that more than one function can be performed, simply by pressing more firmly on the trackpad. It also provides haptic feedback, which is a physical response from the trackpad in the form of a small vibration, once different options have been accessed.

macOS Scroll Bars

In macOS Catalina, scroll bars in web pages and documents are more reactive to the navigational device being used on the computer. By default, with a Magic Trackpad, a trackpad or a Magic Mouse, scroll bars are only visible when scrolling is actually taking place. However, if a mouse is being used they will be visible permanently, although this can be changed for all devices. To perform scrolling with macOS Catalina:

If you do not have a trackpad, a Magic Trackpad or a Magic Mouse you can still navigate in macOS Catalina with a traditional mouse and the use of scroll bars in windows.

1 Scroll around a web page or document by swiping up or down on a Magic Mouse, a Magic Trackpad, or a trackpad. As you move up or down, the scroll bar appears

For instructions on scrolling with a Magic Mouse, see pages 91-92. For scrolling with a Magic Trackpad, see pages 84-85.

2 When you stop scrolling, the bar disappears to allow optimum viewing area for your web page or document

3 To change the scroll bar options, select **System Preferences** > **General** and select the required settings under **Show scroll bars**

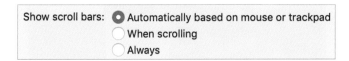

Split View

When working with computers it can sometimes be beneficial to be able to view two windows next to each other. This can be to compare information in two different windows, or just to be able to use two windows without having to access them from the Desktop each time. In macOS Catalina, two windows can be displayed next to each other using the Split View feature:

1 By default, all open windows are layered on top of each other, with the active one at the top

If you click once on the green maximize button this will display the app in full-screen mode, rather than holding on it to activate Split View.

2 Press and hold on the green maximize button and select either **Tile Window to Left of Screen** or **Tile Window to Right of Screen** to position the window accordingly

3 Click on one of the apps on the right-hand side in Step 2 on the previous page to add it as the other Split View panel. Click on each window to make it active

You can work in one panel in Split View (i.e. move through web pages) without affecting the content of the app on the other side.

4 Drag the middle divider bar to resize either of the Split View panels, to change the viewing area

Swap the windows in Split View by dragging the top toolbar of one app into the other window.

5 Move the cursor over the top of the window of each Split View item to view its toolbar and controls

Trackpad Gestures

Pointing and clicking

A Magic Trackpad, or trackpad, can be used to perform a variety of pointing and clicking tasks:

By default, the iMac with Retina Display comes with a Magic Mouse provided. However, this can be swapped for a Magic Trackpad, or both can be included for an additional cost.

1 Tap with one finger in the middle of the Magic Trackpad or trackpad, to perform a single-click operation; e.g. to click on a button or click on an open window

2 Tap once with two fingers in the middle of the Magic Trackpad or trackpad, to access any contextual menus associated with an item (this is the equivalent of the traditional right-click with a mouse)

3 Press and hold with one finger to access data detectors for selected items. This is a content-specific function depending on the selected item: if it is a web page link it will show it in a pop-up window; if it is a calendar-related word – e.g. "tomorrow" – it will create a new calendar event; for other words it will display a definition

Beware

If you have too many functions set using the same number of fingers, some of them may not work. See pages 93-94 for details about setting preferences for Multi-Touch Gestures.

4 Swipe left with three fingers from the right-hand edge of the Magic Trackpad or trackpad to access the Notification Center

...cont'd

Scrolling and zooming

One of the most common operations on a computer is scrolling on a page, whether it is a web page or a document. Traditionally, this has been done with a mouse and a cursor. However, using a Magic Trackpad you can now do all of your scrolling with your fingers. There are a number of options for doing this.

Scrolling up and down

To move up and down web pages or documents, use two fingers on the Magic Trackpad or trackpad, and swipe up or down. The page moves in the opposite direction to the one in which you are swiping – i.e. if you swipe up, the page moves down; and vice versa.

Don't worry if you cannot immediately get the hang of Multi-Touch Gestures. It takes a bit of practice to get the correct touch and pressure on the Magic Trackpad, trackpad or Magic Mouse.

 Open a web page

 Position two fingers in the middle of the Magic Trackpad or trackpad

3 Swipe them up to move down the page

Don't forget

When scrolling up and down pages, the gesture moves the page the opposite way – i.e. swipe down to move up the page; and vice versa.

4 Swipe them down to move up the page

...cont'd

Zooming in and out
To zoom in or out on web pages or documents:

1 To zoom in, position your thumb and forefinger in the middle of the Magic Trackpad or trackpad

Don't forget

Pages can also be zoomed in on by double-tapping with two fingers.

2 Spread them outwards to zoom in on a web page or document

3 To zoom out, position your thumb and forefinger at opposite corners of the Magic Trackpad or trackpad

There is a limit on how far you can zoom in or out on a web page or document, to ensure that it does not distort the content too much.

4 Pinch them into the center of the Magic Trackpad or trackpad, to zoom out

...cont'd

Moving between pages

With Multi-Touch Gestures, it is possible to swipe between pages within a document (such as a book). To do this:

1 Position two fingers to the left or right of the Magic Trackpad or trackpad

2 Swipe to the opposite side of the Magic Trackpad or trackpad, to move through the document

See pages 100-101 for details about using full-screen apps.

88

Moving between full-screen apps

In addition to moving between pages by swiping, it is also possible to move between different apps when they are in full-screen mode. To do this:

1 Position three fingers to the left or right of the Magic Trackpad or trackpad

2 Swipe to the opposite side of the Magic Trackpad or trackpad, to move through the available full-screen apps

Showing the Desktop

To show the whole Desktop, regardless of how many files or apps are open:

1 Position your thumb and three fingers in the middle of the Magic Trackpad or trackpad

2 Swipe to the opposite corners of the Magic Trackpad or trackpad, to display the Desktop

3 The Desktop is displayed, with all items minimized around the side of the screen

Magic Mouse Gestures

Pointing and clicking

A Magic Mouse can be used to perform a variety of pointing and clicking tasks:

Don't forget

The latest version of the Magic Mouse is Magic Mouse 2.

1 Click with one finger on the Magic Mouse to perform a single-click operation; e.g. to select a button or command

Don't forget

The right-click operation can be set within the Mouse System Preferences.

2 Tap with one finger on the right side of the Magic Mouse to access any contextual menus associated with an item (this is the equivalent of the traditional right-click with a mouse)

Scrolling and zooming

The Magic Mouse can also be used to perform scrolling and zooming functions within a web page or document:

1 Swipe up or down with one finger to move up or down a web page or document

Don't forget

When scrolling on a web page or document, it moves in the opposite direction to the movement of your finger – i.e. if you swipe up, the page moves down; and vice versa.

2 Double-tap with one finger to zoom in on a web page

...cont'd

3 Swipe left or right with one finger to move between pages

4 Swipe left or right with two fingers to move between full-screen apps

Multi-Touch Preferences

Some Multi-Touch Gestures only have a single action, which cannot be changed. However, others have options for changing the action linked to a specific gesture. This is done within the respective preferences for the Magic Mouse, the Magic Trackpad or the trackpad, where a full list of Multi-Touch Gestures is shown. To use these:

1 Access the System Preferences and click on the Mouse or Trackpad button

2 Click on one of the tabs at the top

3 The actions are described on the left, with a graphic explanation on the right

The Magic Trackpad, or trackpad, has three tabbed options within the System Preferences: Point & Click, Scroll & Zoom, and More Gestures. The Magic Mouse has preferences for Point & Click and More Gestures.

4 If there is a Down arrow next to an option, click on it to change the way a gesture is actioned

...cont'd

Trackpad gestures
The full list of trackpad Multi-Touch Gestures, with their default action are (relevant ones for Magic Mouse are in brackets):

Point & Click

- Tap to click – tap once with one finger (same for the Magic Mouse).

- Secondary click – click or tap with two fingers (single-click on the right of the Magic Mouse).

- Look up and data detectors – press and hold with one finger.

Scroll & Zoom

- Scroll direction: natural – with two fingers, content tracks finger movement (one finger with the Magic Mouse).

- Zoom in or out – spread or pinch with two fingers.

- Smart zoom – double-tap with two fingers (double-tap with one finger with the Magic Mouse).

- Rotate – rotate with two fingers.

More Gestures

- Swipe between pages – scroll left or right with two fingers (scroll left or right with one finger with the Magic Mouse).

- Swipe between full-screen apps – swipe left or right with three fingers (swipe left or right with two fingers with the Magic Mouse).

- Swipe left with three fingers from the right-hand edge of the trackpad or Magic Trackpad to access the Notification Center.

- Access Mission Control (see next page) – swipe up with three fingers (double-tap with two fingers with the Magic Mouse).

- App Exposé – swipe down with three fingers.

- Access Launchpad – pinch with thumb and three fingers.

- Show Desktop – spread with thumb and three fingers.

94

Natural scrolling means the page follows the direction of your finger, vertically or horizontally, depending on which way you're scrolling.

Hot tip

Exposé enables you to view all of the active windows that are currently open for a particular app.

Mission Control

Mission Control is a function in macOS Catalina that helps you organize all of your open apps, full-screen apps, and documents. It also enables you to quickly view the Desktop. Within Mission Control there is also Spaces, where you can group similar types of documents together. To use Mission Control:

Don't forget

Click on a window in Mission Control to access it and exit the Mission Control window.

1 Click on this button in the Launchpad, or swipe upwards with three fingers on the Magic Trackpad or trackpad, or double-tap with two fingers on a Magic Mouse

Mission Control

2 All open files and apps are visible via Mission Control

Beware

Any apps or files that have been minimized or closed do not appear within the main Mission Control window. Instead, they are located to the right of the dividing line on the Dock.

95

3 If there is more than one window open for an app they will each be shown separately

4 Move the cursor over the top of the Mission Control window to view the different Spaces (see page 96) and any apps in full-screen mode

Desktop 1   Desktop 2

Hot tip

Drag an open app to the top of the screen to access Mission Control. You can then make an app full-screen from Mission Control by dragging it onto one of the Spaces at the top of the window.

Spaces

The top level of Mission Control contains Spaces, which are new Desktop areas into which you can group certain apps; e.g. the Apple productivity apps such as Pages and Numbers. This means that you can access these apps independently from other open items. This helps to organize your apps and files. To use Spaces:

Don't forget

Preferences for Spaces can be set within the Mission Control System Preferences.

Hot tip

Create different Spaces for different types of content; e.g. one for productivity and one for entertainment.

Don't forget

When you create a new Space it can subsequently be deleted by moving the cursor over it and clicking on the cross at the left-hand corner. Any items that have been added to this Space are returned to the default Desktop Space.

1 Move the cursor over the top right-hand corner of Mission Control and click on the **+** symbol

2 A new **Space** is created along the top row of Mission Control

Desktop 2

3 Drag an app onto the Space, and then any additional apps required

Desktop 2

4 The new Space can then be accessed by clicking on the Space within Mission Control, and all of the apps that have been placed here will be available

5 macOS Catalina Apps

Apps are the programs with which you start putting macOS to use, either for work or for fun. This chapter looks at using apps and the online App Store.

Launchpad

Even though the Dock can be used to store shortcuts to your applications, it is limited in terms of space. The full set of applications on your Mac can be found in the Finder (see Chapter 3) but macOS Catalina has a feature that allows you to quickly access and manage all of your applications. These include the ones that are pre-installed on your Mac and also any that you install yourself or download from the Apple App Store. This feature is called Launchpad. To use it:

Hot tip

If the apps take up more than one screen, swipe from right to left with two fingers to view the additional pages, or click on the dots at the bottom of the window.

1 Click once on this button on the Dock

2 All of the apps (applications) are displayed

Don't forget

To launch an app from within Launchpad, click on it once.

Hot tip

One of the apps in Utilities is Boot Camp Assistant, which can be used to run Windows on your Mac, if required.

3 Similar types of apps can be grouped together in individual folders. By default, the **Other** (**Utilities**) apps are grouped in this way

4 To create a group of similar apps, drag the icon for one over another

5 The apps are grouped together in a folder in Launchpad, with **Untitled** as the default name of the folder

6 To change the name, click on it once and overtype it with the new name

System apps – i.e. the ones that already come with your Mac – cannot be removed in the Launchpad, only ones you have downloaded.

7 The folder appears within the **Launchpad** window

8 To remove an app, click and hold on it until it starts to jiggle and a cross appears. Click on the cross to remove it

Full-screen Apps

When working with apps we all like to be able to see as much of a window as possible. With macOS Catalina this is possible with the full-screen app option. This allows you to expand an app with this functionality so that it takes up the whole of your monitor or screen with a minimum of toolbars visible. Some apps have this functionality but some do not. To use full-screen apps:

1 By default, an app appears on the Desktop with other windows behind it

If the button in Step 2 is not visible then the app does not have the full-screen functionality.

2 Click on this button at the top left-hand corner of the app's window

3 The app is expanded to take up the whole window. The main Apple Menu bar and the Dock are hidden

4   To view the main Menu bar, move the cursor over the top of the screen

5   You can move between all full-screen apps by swiping with three fingers left or right on a trackpad or Magic Mouse

Hot tip

For more information about navigating with Multi-Touch Gestures, see pages 82-94.

6   Move the cursor over the top left-hand corner of the screen and click on this button to close the full-screen functionality

7   In Mission Control all of the open full-screen apps are shown in the top row

macOS Apps

macOS Catalina apps include:

- **Books**. An app for downloading ebooks. (See pages 155-156.)

- **Calculator**. A basic calculator.

- **Calendar**. (See pages 112-113.)

- **Contacts**. (See pages 110-111.)

- **Dictionary**. A digital dictionary.

- **FaceTime**. Can be used for video calls. (See page 142.)

- **Find My**. This can be used to locate missing Apple devices.

- **Home**. This can be used to control compatible smart home devices; e.g. smart lighting and smart heating.

- **Music, TV, Photos and Podcasts**. (See Chapter 8 for details about these apps.)

- **Mail**. The default email app.

- **Maps**. For viewing locations and destinations worldwide.

- **Messages**. (See pages 140-141.)

- **Mission Control**. The function for organizing your Desktop.

- **News**. This aggregates news stories from several sources. (See page 120.)

- **Notes**. (See pages 114-115.)

- **Photo Booth**. An app for creating photo effects.

- **Preview**. (See page 126.)

- **Reminders**. (See pages 116-117.)

- **Safari**. The macOS-specific web browser.

- **Stocks**. This can be used to display stock market information.

- **Time Machine**. macOS's backup facility. (In some instances, this can be located in the Utilities/Other folder.)

- **Voice Memos**. (See page 121.)

The macOS apps can be accessed from the Launchpad and also the Applications folder from within the Finder.

The Music, TV, Podcasts and Find My apps are all new in macOS Catalina.

Some apps are grouped together in the Utilities/Other folder. These include TextEdit, Chess, Stickies, Font Book, QuickTime Player, and Screenshot.

For qualifying Macs with macOS Catalina, the Apple productivity apps (Pages, Numbers and Keynote) are free to download from the App Store, or come pre-installed.

Accessing the App Store

The App Store is another macOS app. This is an online facility where you can download and buy new apps. These cover a range of categories such as productivity, business and entertainment. When you select or buy an app from the App Store, it is downloaded automatically by Launchpad and appears there next to the rest of the apps.

To buy apps from the App Store you need to have an Apple ID. If you have not already set this up, it can be done when you first access the App Store. To use the App Store:

1 Click on this icon on the Dock or within the Launchpad

2 The Homepage of the App Store contains the current top featured and best new apps

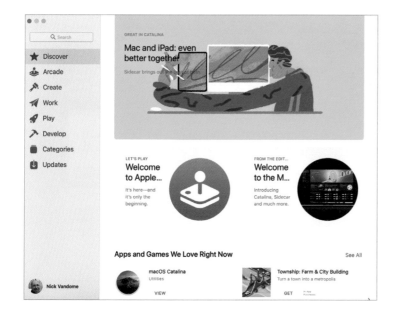

3 Your account information and quick links to other areas of the App Store are listed at the left-hand side of the page

Click on the **Arcade** button in the left-hand sidebar to access the Arcade option for playing games. This is a subscription service (with a one-month free trial) that gives unlimited access to original Apple games that can be played on your own, or with other people. It can also be used with Family Sharing. This is a new feature in macOS Catalina.

By default, the App Store opens at the Homepage, which is accessed by clicking on the **Discover** button in the left-hand sidebar.

Downloading Apps

The App Store contains a wide range of apps: from small, fun apps to powerful productivity ones. However, downloading them from the App Store is the same regardless of the type of app. The only differences are whether they need to be paid for or not and the length of time they take to download. To download an app from the App Store:

1 Browse through the App Store until you find the required app

2 Click on the app to view a detailed description about it

Hot tip

When downloading apps, start with a free one first so that you can get used to the process before you download paid-for apps.

3 Click on the button next to the app icon to download it. If the app is free the button will say **Get**

4 If there is a charge (displayed in local currency) for the app, the button will say **Buy App** once the price is clicked

5 Click on the **Install** button

6 Enter your **Apple ID** account details to continue downloading the app and click on the **Get** button

Depending on their size, different apps take differing amounts of time to be downloaded.

7 The progress of the download is displayed in a progress bar underneath the Launchpad icon on the Dock

8 Once it has been downloaded, the app is available within the Launchpad

As you download more apps, additional pages will be created within the Launchpad to accommodate them.

Finding Apps

There are thousands of apps in the App Store and sometimes the hardest task is locating the ones you want. However, there are a number of ways in which finding apps is made as easy as possible:

1 Click on the **Discover** button

2 The main window has a range of suggested apps. Scroll down the page to see a panel with the current **Top Free** apps and games

3 Underneath this is a list of the current **Top Paid** apps and games

The Top Charts has sections for paid-for apps and free ones.

4 Click on the **See All** button to view the full list of Top Charts apps

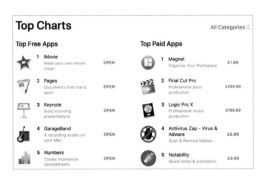

...cont'd

5 Click on the buttons in the left-hand panel to view the available apps with them

6 Each heading contains relevant apps

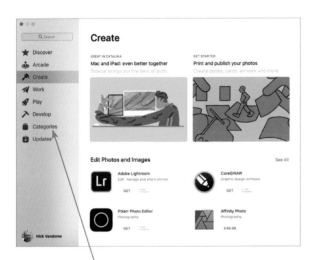

Another way to find apps is to type a keyword into the Search box at the top left-hand corner of the App Store window.

7 Click on the **Categories** button

8 Browse through the apps by specific categories, such as Business, Entertainment and Finance

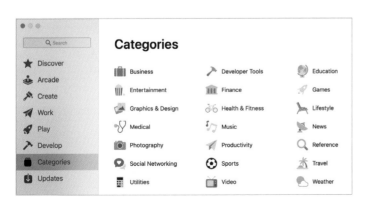

Managing Your Apps

Once you have bought apps from the App Store you can view details of ones you have purchased and also install updated versions of them. To view your purchased apps:

Don't forget

Even if you interrupt a download and turn off your Mac you will still be able to resume the download when you restart your computer.

1 Click on your own account name, in the bottom left-hand corner

2 Details of your purchased apps are displayed (including those that are free)

Updating apps

Improvements and fixes are being developed constantly, and these can be downloaded to ensure that all of your apps are up-to-date:

1 When updates are available this is indicated by a red circle on the App Store icon on the Dock

Hot tip

Apps can also be updated automatically. This can be specified in **System Preferences** > **Software Update** > **Advanced**. Check **On** the **Download new updates when available** option. Underneath this there are options for downloading and installing updates.

2 Click on the **Updates** button

3 Information about the update is displayed next to the app that is due to be updated

4 Click on the **Update** button to update an individual app

5 Click on the **Update All** button to update all of the apps that are due to be updated

6 Getting Productive

There are several built-in apps within macOS Catalina that can be used to create, store and display information for use every day. This chapter shows how to access and use these apps, so that you can make the most of macOS Catalina as an effective and efficient productivity tool.

Contacts (Address Book)

The Contacts app can be used to store contact information, which can then be used in different apps and shared via iCloud. To view contacts:

Hot tip

Contacts can be shared by clicking on the **Share** button and selecting one of the available options.

 Open **Contacts** from this address book icon, and click on one of the contacts in the left-hand panel to view their details

Adding contact information

The main function of the Contacts app is to store details of personal and business contacts. Contacts must be added manually for each entry, but it can prove to be a valuable resource once this has been completed. To add contact information:

Hot tip

Click on the **Edit** button to edit a contact's details.

Edit

1 Click on this button to add a new contact

2 Click on a category, and enter contact information. Press the **Tab** key to move to the next field

3 Click on the **Done** button once you have completed the entry

Creating groups

In addition to creating individual entries in the Contacts app, group contacts can also be created. This is a way of grouping contacts with similar interests or connections. Once a group has been created, all of the entries within it can be accessed and contacted by selecting the relevant entry in the left-hand panel. To create a group:

1 Select **File** > **New Group** from the Menu bar to create a new group entry

2 Give the new group a name

3 Drag individual entries into the group (the individual entries are retained, too)

4 Click on a group name to view the members of the group

Individuals can be included in several groups. If you change their details in one group, these changes will take effect across all of the groups in which the entry occurs.

111

Groups in the Contacts app can be used to send group emails; i.e. you can type the name of the group into the **Mail To** box to generate the names in the group, and then send the email to all of these recipients.

Calendar

Electronic calendars are now a standard part of modern life, and with macOS this function is performed by the Calendar app. Not only can this be used on your Mac; it can also be synchronized with other Apple devices such as an iPad or an iPhone, using iCloud. To create a calendar:

The Calendar app displays the current date in the icon on the Dock.

1 Click on this icon on the Dock, or in the Launchpad

2 Select whether to view the calendar by Day, Week, Month or Year

Day	Week	Month	Year

3 In Month view, the current day is denoted by a red circle on the date

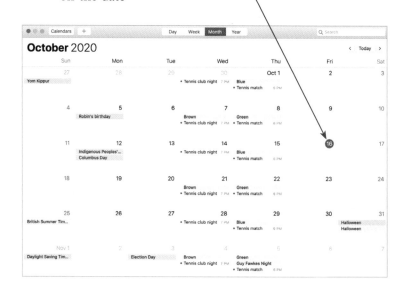

Click on the **Today** button to view the current day. Click on the Forward or Back arrows to move to the next day, week, month or year, depending on what is selected in Step 2.

If Family Sharing has been activated, the Family calendar will automatically be added for all members of the Family Sharing group.

4 Scroll up and down to move through the weeks and months. In macOS Catalina this is done with continuous scrolling, which means you can view weeks across different months; i.e. you can view the second half of one month and the first half of the next one in the same window

Adding events

1 Select a date and double-click on it; or **Ctrl + click** on the date, then select **New Event**

2 Click on the **New Event** field and enter an event name

3 Click on the date or time to amend it by entering new details. Check **On** the **all-day** box to set the event for a whole day

Finding locations
When adding events you can also find details about locations:

1 Click on the **Add Location** field, and start typing a destination name or zip (postal) code. Suggestions will appear underneath, including matching items from your contacts list. Click on a location to select it

2 A map of the location is displayed, including a real-time weather summary for the location. Click on the map to view it in greater detail in the **Maps** app

Click on this button on the Menu bar to add a **Quick Event**, with just one text box for all of the relevant information. Once it has been added it can then be edited like a regular event by double-clicking on it.

Other items that can be included in an event are: inviting people to it; calculating the travel time from your current location; creating a repeat event; and setting an alert for it.

113

Taking Notes

It is always useful to have a quick way of making notes of everyday things such as shopping lists, recipes or packing lists for traveling. With macOS Catalina, the Notes app is perfect for this task. To use it:

Click on this button on the top toolbar to view the Notes Homepage as a gallery of thumbnails, rather than the default list option. This makes it easier to identify specific lists and their content. This is a new feature in macOS Catalina.

1 Click on this icon on the Dock, or in the Launchpad

2 The right-hand panel is where the note is created. The middle panel displays a list of all notes

Enable iCloud for Notes so that all of your notes will be backed up, and also available on all of your iCloud-enabled devices. You will also be able to access them by signing in to your account with your Apple ID at www.icloud.com

3 Click on this button to show or hide the left-hand panel in the Notes app, which displays the notes folders

4 Click on this button to add a new note

5 As more notes are added, the most recent appears at the top of the list in the middle panel. Double-click the new note to add text and edit formatting options (see next page)

The first line of a note becomes its heading in the notes panel.

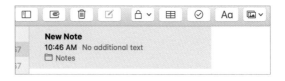

Formatting notes

In macOS Catalina there are a number of formatting options for the Notes app:

1 Enter a line of text, and click on this button to add a check button

Hot tip

Click on this button to add a table to a note.

2 Click on the check button to add a check mark, to indicate that an item has been completed

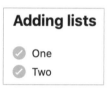

Don't forget

Click on the **Share** button to share a note with other people, via a range of other apps.

3 Highlight a piece of text, and click on this button to access formatting options for it

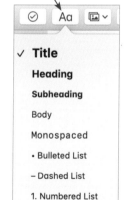

Click on this button to invite other people to have access to the note so they can view it and edit it.

4 Click on this button on the Notes toolbar to add photos and videos, sketches, scans, maps, websites, sound clips and documents to a note. Navigate to the required item and drag it into the note from the Attachments Browser

Hot tip

Content can be added to notes from a range of other apps, such as Safari or the Photos app, by clicking on the **Share** button in the relevant app and selecting **Notes** as the option.

Setting Reminders

Another useful app for keeping organized is Reminders. This enables you to create lists for different topics and also set reminders for specific items. A date and time can be set for each reminder, and when this is reached, the reminder appears on your Mac screen (and in the Notification Center). To use Reminders:

The Reminders app has been updated in macOS Catalina.

1 Click on this icon on the Dock, or in the Launchpad

2 The Reminders window contains a **My Lists** section where lists and reminders are created and a Smart Lists section, at the top of the left-hand sidebar, where matching items are collated

As with Notes, iCloud makes your reminders available on all of your Apple devices; i.e. your Mac, iPad, iPhone and iPod Touch.

3 Click on the one of the **My Lists** options; e.g. **Reminders** option

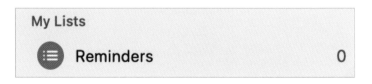

4 Click on this button to add a new reminder +

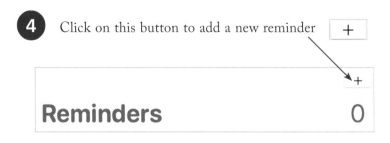

5 Enter the title of the reminder and tap once on the **i** button to access the **Details** window

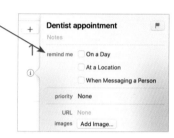

6 Next to the **remind me** heading are options that can be added to the reminder, such as being reminded on specific date, at a location or when messaging someone

Hot tip

If the **On a Day** option is selected in Step 7, a **repeat** option then becomes available. This can be used to create a recurring reminder. The options for this are **None**, **Every Day**, **Every Week**, **Every Month** or **Every Year**, or **Custom...**.

7 Check **On** the **On a Day** option and select a specific day from the calendar

8 The reminder is created, with any criteria, such as date, listed on the reminder

Hot tip

Click on other options in Step 8 – e.g. **Add Time** or **Add Location** – to include these in the reminder.

9 Items are listed below the relevant headings under **My Lists**, and also in the Smart Lists section. New lists in each category will automatically appear in each section

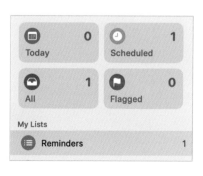

Notifications

The Notification Center provides a single location to view all of your emails, messages, updates and alerts. Notifications appear at the top right-hand corner of the screen. The items that appear in Notifications are set up within System Preferences. To do this:

1 Open System Preferences and click on the **Notifications** button

2 The items that will appear in the Notification Center are listed here. Click on an item to select it and set its notification options

3 To disable an item so that it does not appear in the Notification Center, select it as above and check **Off** the **Show in Notification Center** box

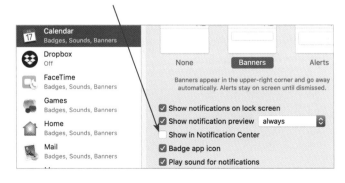

Viewing notifications

Notifications appear in the Notification Center. The way they appear can be determined in System Preferences:

1 Select an alert style. A banner alert comes up on the screen and then disappears after a few seconds

2 The **Alerts** option shows the notification, and it stays on screen until dismissed (such as this one for reminders)

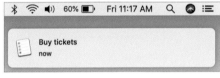

3 Click on this button in the top right-hand corner of the screen to view all of the items in the Notification Center. Click on it again to hide the Notification Center

4 In the Notification Center, click on the **Today** button to view the weather forecast, calendar events and stock market reports for the current day. Click on the **Edit** button at the bottom to change the items that appear

5 Click on the **Notifications** button to view the items that have been set up to appear here. Items such as emails and iMessages can be replied to directly by clicking on them from within the Notifications section

Hot tip

The Notification Center can also be displayed using a trackpad or Magic Trackpad by dragging with three fingers from right to left, starting from the far right edge.

Don't forget

Software updates can also appear in the Notification Center, when they are available.

News

The News app has been a regular feature on Apple's mobile devices for a number of years. It is now available on Macs using macOS Catalina. To use it:

1 Click on the **News** app

2 Click on the **Today** button in the left-hand panel to view the latest stories in your news feed

3 Click on the **More Top Stories** link to view the top items recommended by Apple News (based on your own news selections)

4 On the News app Menu bar, select **File > Discover Channels & Topics...** to view subjects or publications which you are following; i.e. they are used to populate your news feed

5 In the **Channels & Topics** section, click on items to select them and add them as topics or publications that are added as favorites on your Today page

Hot tip

Click on the **Spotlight** button in the left-hand panel to view in-depth features about topics in which you are interested.

Voice Memos

Voice memos are an increasingly popular way to send short voice messages to family and friends. They can also be used as a method of verbal note-taking, when you want to remember something. To use voice memos:

1 Click on the **Voice Memos** app

2 Click on the red **Record** button to start recording a voice memo

3 Click on this button to finish recording

4 Click on the **Done** button to save the recording

5 The latest recording is placed at the top of the list in the left-hand panel of the Voice Memos app

6 Click on a memo to display it in the main window. Click on the **Play** button to hear the recording

7 Click on the **Edit** button in the top right-hand corner of the main window to amend a voice memo

Hot tip

In the **Edit** window, click on the **Crop** button and drag the yellow handles left or right to trim the duration of a voice memo. Tap on the **Trim** button below the yellow handles to complete the operation. This is a good option if there are pauses at the beginning or the end of the recording.

Getting Around with Maps

With the Maps app you need never again wonder about where a location is, or worry about getting directions to somewhere. Using Maps with macOS Catalina, you will be able to do the following:

- Search maps from around the world

- Find addresses

- Find famous buildings or landmarks

- Get directions between different locations

- View transit information for a route

- View traffic conditions

Viewing maps

Enable **Location Services** and then you can start looking around maps, from the viewpoint of your current location.

Don't forget

Location Services can be enabled in **System Preferences** > **Security & Privacy**. Click on the **Privacy** tab, click on **Location Services** and check on the **Enable Location Services** checkbox. (You may need to click the lock in the bottom-left corner and enter your sign-in password before you can make any changes.) Maps can be used without Location Services but this would mean that Maps cannot use your current location or determine information in relation to this.

1 Click on this button on the Dock or in the Launchpad

2 Click on this button to view your current location

3 Double-click to zoom in on the map. Press **Option + double-click** to zoom out. Or, swipe outwards with thumb and forefinger to zoom in, and pinch inwards to zoom out

4 Or, click on these buttons to zoom in and out on a map and also view it in 3D

Finding locations

Locations in Maps can be found for addresses, cities or landmarks. To find items in Maps:

1 Enter a term into the Search box and click on one of the results

2 The selected item is displayed and shown on a map. Pins are also dropped at this point to mark the location

3 Click on one of the buttons on the top Maps toolbar to view **Map**, **Transit** or **Satellite** views of the location

4 Click on the pin on the map to select the location

5 Click here to view more details about the location, including options for adding it to contact information and getting directions to the location. You can also access a **Flyover Tour** of the location (if available)

Hot tip

Click on the 3D button to change the perspective of the map being viewed. Rotate your fingers on the trackpad to change the orientation of the map.

Don't forget

Flyover Tour (if available for a location) provides an animated 3D experience that travels through the most notable sights for that location.

Don't forget

Click on this button in Step 2 to swap the locations for which you want directions.

Don't forget

Click on the **Walk** button in Step 2 to view the directions by foot instead of by car.

Hot tip

Click on the **Share** button to send the directions to a mobile device, such as an iPhone or an iPad, so that you can follow the directions on the go.

...cont'd

Getting directions

Within Maps you can also get directions to most locations.

1 Click on the **Directions** button

Directions

2 By default, your current location is used for the **Start** field. If you want to change this, click once and enter a new location

3 Enter an **End** location or address

4 Click on one of the options for reaching your destination (**Drive**, **Walk** or **Transit**). The route is shown on the map, with the directions down the left-hand side of the window. The default mode of transport is for driving

5 Click in the **Show** box to view the map in 3D, or for Traffic, which shows any traffic disruption

Finding transit directions

In macOS Catalina there is an option for accessing transit options between two locations. To do this:

1 Enter the two locations, as shown on the previous page. Click on the **Transit** button

2 The transit options are shown in the left-hand panel

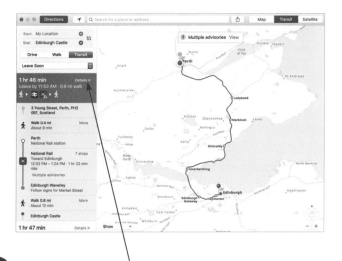

3 Click on the **Details** button next to an option to view its full details. This will include any parts of the journey where you will have to walk between the transit services required for your journey

Hot tip

Click on the **Leave Soon** box in Step 1 to specify a time for when your journey will be taking place. The transit details will be updated according to your leaving time.

Don't forget

The Transit option is only available for a limited number of locations around the world; the majority being in the US.

Preview

Preview is a macOS app that can be used to view multiple file types, particularly image file formats. This can be useful if you just want to view documents without editing them in a dedicated app, such as an image-editing app. Preview in macOS Catalina can also be used to store and view documents in iCloud.

To open Preview, click on this icon in the Applications folder in the Finder, or in the Launchpad:

Preview

1 Open Preview and click on one of the options in the Finder sidebar

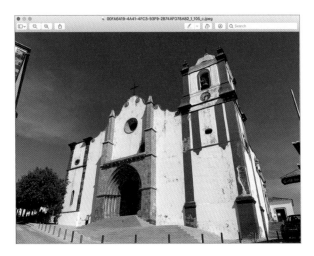

Preview is also a good option for viewing PDF (Portable Document Format) documents.

2 Double-click on an item to view it at full size. This can be from any of the folders within the Finder. The item is opened in the Preview window

Printing

macOS Catalina makes the printing process as simple as possible, partly by its ability to automatically install new printers as soon as they are connected to your Mac. However, it is also possible to install printers manually. To do this:

1 Open **System Preferences** and click on the **Printers & Scanners** button

Printers & Scanners

2 Currently-installed printers are displayed in the Printers list. Click here to add a new printer

3 Select an available printer

Name
Dell Laser Printer 1720dn

4 Click on the **Add** button to load the printer drivers for the selected printer

Add

5 The printer drivers are added

Setting up 'Dell Laser Printer 1720dn...'

Setting up the device...

Configure   Cancel

6 The printer is added in the **Printers & Scanners** window, under the **Printers** list, ready for use

For most printers, macOS will detect them when they are first connected, and they should be ready to use without the need to install any software or apply new settings.

127

Once a printer has been installed, documents can be printed by selecting **File** > **Print** from the Menu bar. Print settings can be set at this point, and they can also be set by selecting **File** > **Page/Print Setup** from the Menu bar in most apps.

macOS Utilities

In addition to the apps in the Applications folder, there are also a number of utility apps that perform a variety of tasks within macOS. (Some of the utilities vary depending on the hardware setup of your Mac.) The utility apps are in the **Other** folder:

Don't forget

The Utilities folder is also available from within the Applications folder. On some systems it may appear as "Other" in the Launchpad.

 1 Access the Launchpad to access the Other folder. The utilities are displayed within the Other folder

Other

- **Activity Monitor**. This contains information about the system memory being used and disk activity (see page 180 for more details).

- **AirPort Utility**. This sets up the AirPort wireless networking facility that can be used to connect to the internet with a Wi-Fi connection.

- **Audio MIDI Setup**. This can be used for adding audio devices and setting their properties.

- **Automator**. This can be used to create automated tasks.

- **Bluetooth File Exchange**. This determines how files are exchanged between your computer and other Bluetooth devices (if this function is enabled).

- **Boot Camp Assistant**. This can be used to run Windows operating systems on your Mac.

- **Chess**. A game that can be played against your Mac.

- **ColorSync Utility**. This can be used to view and create color profiles on your computer. These can then be used by apps to try to match output color with monitor color.

- **Console**. This displays the behind-the-scenes messages that are being passed around the computer while its usual tasks are being performed.

- **Digital Color Meter**. This can be used to measure the exact color values of a particular color.

- **Disk Utility**. This can be used to view details about attached disks and repair errors (see page 178 for more details).

Don't forget

The utilities are the workhorses of macOS. They do not have the glamour of apps such as the Music app, but they perform vital gathering of information and general maintenance tasks.

Don't forget

You may never need to use a utility like the Console, but it is worth having a look at it just to see the inner workings of a computer.

- **Feedback Assistant**. This can be used to receive and send feedback updates about Apple and macOS.

- **Font Book**. This displays the available system fonts.

- **Grapher**. This is a utility for creating simple or more complex scientific graphs.

- **Image Capture**. This can be used to capture images, or transfer and scan images.

- **Keychain Access**. This can be used to manage passwords for websites and also create new secure passwords as required.

- **Migration Assistant**. This helps in the transfer of files between two Mac computers. This can be used if you buy a new Mac and you need to transfer files from another one.

- **QuickTime Player**. This can be used to play video files.

- **Screenshot**. This is a utility that can be used to capture screenshots, which are images of the screen at a given point in time. You can grab different portions of the screen, including timed options.

- **Script Editor**. This can be used to create your own scripts with Apple's dedicated scripting app, AppleScript.

- **Stickies**. This can be used to attach short notes to the screen.

- **System Information**. This contains details of the hardware devices and software applications that are installed on your computer (see page 179 for more details).

- **Terminal**. Within the Terminal you can view the workings of UNIX and also start to write your own apps, if you have some UNIX programming knowledge.

- **TextEdit**. This is a basic word processing app.

- **Time Machine**. This is the macOS backup facility.

- **VoiceOver Utility**. This has various options for how the VoiceOver function works within macOS. This is the digital voice that can be used to read out what is on the screen, and it is particularly useful for users who are visually impaired.

Hot tip

The Screenshot utility is a feature that is useful if you are producing manuals or books, and need to display examples of a screen or app.

Creating PDF Documents

PDF (Portable Document Format) is a file format that preserves the formatting of an original document, and it can also be viewed on a variety of computer platforms including Mac, Windows and UNIX. macOS has a built-in PDF function that can produce PDF files from many apps. To do this:

PDF files can be viewed with the Preview app.

1 Open a file in an app and select **File > Export as PDF...**,

or use the **File > Save As...** option, and change the format of the document to PDF, where offered

2 Browse to a destination for the file, and click **Save**

PDF is an excellent option if you are creating documents such as instruction booklets, magazines or manuals.

3 Locate the selected destination to view and open the newly-created PDF file. You can then access options for viewing, sharing or marking up the document

Algarve church

7 Internet and Email

This chapter shows how to get the most out of the internet and email. It covers how to use and customize the macOS web browser, Safari, and its email app, Mail. It also covers Messages for text messaging, and video calling.

About Safari

Safari is a web browser that is designed specifically to be used with macOS. It is similar in most respects to other browsers, but it usually functions more quickly with macOS.

Safari overview

Don't forget

Before you connect to the internet you must have an Internet Service Provider (ISP) who will provide you with the relevant method of connection; e.g. cable, wireless or dial-up (if being used). They will also provide you with any passwords (for connecting to a Wi-Fi router) and login details. Click on the **Network** option in System Preferences to view the available networks.

Network

1 Click here on the Dock to launch Safari

2 All of the controls are at the top of the browser

Toolbar   Address Bar/Search Box   Tabs

Favorites Bar   Main content area

Address Bar/Search Box

In Safari, the Address Bar and the Search Box is combined, and can be used for searching for an item or entering a web address to go to that page:

Hot tip

If the Favorites Bar is not visible, select **View** from the Menu bar and check on the **Show Favorites Bar** option. From this menu you can also select or deselect items such as showing the sidebar, the Status Bar and the Reading List. You can also display the sidebar by clicking on the Show sidebar button.

1 Click in the Address Bar/Search Box

2 Type a website address or a keyword. As you type, suggestions appear below the Address Bar/Search Box. Click on the **Top Hit** option to go to that website

132

Start Page

When you first open Safari, or open a new tab, the Start page is displayed. This can contain a selection of items that can be set within the Safari Preferences. By default, it shows the favorites pages, frequently-visited pages and items selected by Siri.

1 The Start page is used when Safari is opened, or when a new tab is opened

2 Click on the **Show More** button to show more favorite sites on the Start page

By default, the items displayed on the Start page consist of Favorites but this can be customized. To do this:

1 Select **Safari > Preferences...** from the Safari Menu bar

2 Click on the **General** tab for accessing options for how the Start page operates

3 Click here next to **New windows open with** to select options for what appears on the Start page

The Safari Start page has been updated in macOS Catalina, to include Siri suggestions based on other items that you have looked at, in Safari and other apps.

Hot tip

The **General** Safari Preferences can also be used to specify what appears when a new tab is opened, from the **New tabs open with** option. These are the same options as those in Step 3.

Hot tip

A specific page (Homepage) can also be set as the option when a new window or a new tab is opened. The Homepage can be set in the **General** Safari Preferences from the **Homepage** option.

Safari Sidebar

A useful feature in Safari is the Safari sidebar. This is a panel in which you can view all of your Bookmarks and Reading List items, which can be read when the Mac is offline.

Hot tip

If you have an iPhone you can use your Mac and macOS Catalina to create a Personal Hotspot, so that you can use the cellular data connection from your iPhone as a Wi-Fi connection for your Mac (using your iPhone data allowance), if you cannot use your own Wi-Fi connection or you are away from home.

To do this, both devices have to be signed in to the same iCloud account. Click on the Wi-Fi icon at the right-hand side of the top Menu bar and select your iPhone from the Wi-Fi menu. This will give you online access and you can reconnect to the Hotspot the next time that you want to use it, as long as your iPhone is near your Mac.

134

1 Select **View** > **Show Sidebar** from the Safari Menu bar, or click on this button

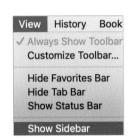

2 Click on the **Bookmarks** button to view all of the items that you have bookmarked (see page 136). Click on the plus symbol **+** at the bottom of the sidebar panel to add more folders for your bookmarks

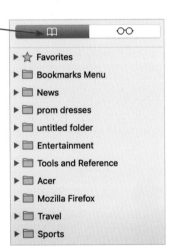

3 Click on the **Reading List** button to view all of the items that you have added to your Reading List so that they can be read later, even if you are offline and not connected to the internet. These can be added from the **Share** button

Safari Tabbed Browsing

Tabs are now a familiar feature on web browsers, so you can have multiple sites open within the same browser window:

1 When more than one tab is open, the tabs appear at the top of the web pages

2 Click on this button on the far right of the tabs to open a new tab

3 Click on one of the **Favorites** or **Frequently Visited** sites listed, or enter a website address in the Address Bar

4 Click on this button next to the New Tab button to minimize all of the current tabs

5 Move left and right to view all of the open tabs in thumbnail view. Click on one to view it at full size

Don't forget

Safari is a full-screen app and can be expanded by clicking the green button in the top left-hand corner. For more information on full-screen apps, see pages 100-101.

Hot tip

Select **Safari** > **Preferences** from the Menu bar to specify settings for the way Safari operates.

Don't forget

If you have open tabs on other Apple devices (e.g. other Mac computers, iPads or iPhones) these will be listed at the bottom of the window in Step 5. Click on an item to open it in Safari on your Mac.

Adding Bookmarks

Bookmarks is a feature with which you can create quick links to your favorite web pages or the ones you visit most frequently. Bookmarks can be added to a menu or the Bookmarks panel in Safari, which makes them even quicker to access. Folders can also be created to store the less frequently-used bookmarks. To view and create bookmarks:

1 Click on this button to view the sidebar

2 Click on this button to view the bookmarks. All of the saved bookmarks can be accessed from here

3 Click on the **Share** button, and click on the **Add Bookmark** button to create a bookmark for the page currently being viewed

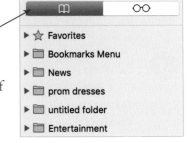

4 Enter a name for the bookmark and select a location for it

5 Click on the **Add** button

Hot tip

Bookmarks can be added to the Favorites Bar, which can be displayed at the top of the Safari window, below the Address Bar. To add bookmarks to the Favorites Bar, select **Favorites** for **Add this page to:** in Step 4. To show (or hide) the Favorites Bar, select **View** > **Show Favorites Bar** (or **Hide Favorites Bar**) from the Safari Menu bar. The Favorites folder is displayed at the top of the Bookmarks panel.

Website Settings

One of the most annoying things about using the web is the adverts that seem to appear by coincidence when you are browsing a website. These are actually based on items that you have previously looked at on the web, and are generated by cookies that have been downloaded from the original site. However, with macOS Catalina a lot of these adverts are blocked automatically, and you can also apply your own settings for specific pages to enable or restrict certain items.

1 Select **Safari** > **Settings for This Website...** from the Safari Menu bar

2 Make selections as required, such as enabling the Reader function and using content blockers. Click on the **Enable content blockers** option to block unwanted items

The Reader function is one where a web page can be read without additional items such as toolbars, buttons and navigation bars. If a page supports the Reader function it will display this button in the Address Bar.

3 Select **Safari** > **Preferences...** from the Safari Menu bar, and click on the Privacy button on the top toolbar

4 Under **Website tracking**, check **On** the **Prevent cross-site tracking** checkbox to prevent websites displaying adverts based on what you have viewed on other sites

Mail

Email is an essential element for most computer users, and Macs come with their own email app called Mail. This covers all of the email functionality that most people could need.

When first using Mail, you have to set up your email account. This can be done with most email accounts and also a wide range of webmail accounts, including iCloud. To add email accounts:

Don't forget

Mail is a full-screen app. For more information on full-screen apps, see pages 100-101.

Don't forget

You can set up more than one account in the Mail app and you can download messages from all of the accounts that you set up. To set up an account from the Mail app, select **Mail** > **Add Account** from the Menu bar.

Don't forget

Emails can be searched for using the Search box in the Mail app. Matching items are grouped according to People, Subjects and Attachments.

1 Click on this icon on the Dock

2 Check on the button next to the type of account that you want to add to the Mail app; e.g. if you have an iCloud account, select iCloud to add this

3 Enter details of the account, and click on the **Next** button

4 Check the **Mail** option for iCloud to sync your iCloud email across any other Apple devices and also your online account at **www.icloud.com**

Using Mail

Mail enables you to send and receive emails, and also format them to your own style. This can be simply formatting text, or attaching images or documents. To use Mail:

1 Click on the **Get Mail** button to download available email messages

2 Click on the **New Message** button to create a new email

3 Click on these buttons to **Reply** to, **Reply** (to) **All**, or **Forward** an email you have received

4 Select or open an email, and click on the **Trash** button to delete it

5 Click on the **Junk** button to mark an email as junk or spam. This trains Mail to identify junk mail. After a period of time, these types of messages will automatically be moved straight into the Junk mailbox

6 Click on the **Format** button to access options for formatting the text in the email

7 Use these buttons in the New Message window to select fonts and font size; color; bold; italic; underlining; strikethrough; and alignment options

8 Click on the **Attach** button to browse your folders to include a file in your email. This can be items such as photos, Word documents or PDF files

Hot tip

To show the descriptive text underneath an icon in Mail, **Ctrl** + **click** next to an icon and select **Icon and Text** from the menu.

Hot tip

When entering the name of a recipient for a message, Mail will display details of matching names from the Contacts app. For instance, if you type "DA", all of the entries in your Contacts beginning with this will be displayed, and you can then select the required one.

Hot tip

If you forward an email with an attachment, then the attachment is included. If you reply to an email, the attachment will not be included.

Messaging

The Messages app enables you to send text messages (iMessages) to other macOS Catalina users or those with an iPhone, iPad or iPod Touch using iOS. It can also be used to send photos and videos, and to make FaceTime calls. To use Messages:

Don't forget

iMessages are specific to Apple and sent over Wi-Fi. SMS (Short Message Service) messages are usually sent between cellular devices, such as smartphones, that are contracted to a compatible mobile services provider.

1 Click on this icon on the Dock

2 You need an Apple ID to use Messages, and you will need to enter these details when you first access it. If you do not have an Apple ID you will be able to create one at this point

3 Click on this button to start a new conversation

4 Click on this button and select a contact (these will be from your Contacts app). To send an iMessage, the recipient must have an Apple ID

Hot tip

Photos and videos can be added to an iMessage by selecting them in the Finder and dragging them into the text box within the Messages app.

5 The person with whom you are having a conversation is displayed in the left-hand panel. The conversation continues down the right-hand panel

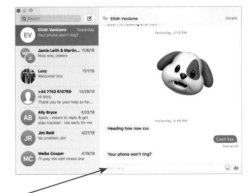

6 Click here to write a message, and press **Return** to send

7 Click on this button at the right-hand side of the text box to access the range of emojis (small graphical symbols)

8 Click on an emoji to add it to a message

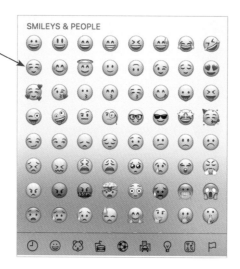

9 Scroll down the window to view all of the emojis, or click on the bottom toolbar to move through the categories

10 Some emojis of people have options to select different styles. Click and hold on a relevant item to view the options. Click on one to add it to a message

To delete a conversation, hover over it in the left-hand panel and click on this cross.

Hot tip

Audio messages can also be included in an iMessage. Click on this icon to the right of the text box, and record your message.

141

Don't forget

Messages in macOS also supports Tapback, whereby you can add an icon to a message as a quick reply. To do this, click and hold on a message text and click on an icon.

FaceTime

FaceTime is an app that can be used to make video and audio calls to other Macs, iPhones, iPads and iPod Touches. To use FaceTime on your Mac you must have an in-built FaceTime camera, or use a compatible external one. To use FaceTime:

Hot tip

macOS on a Mac can be used for phone call forwarding from your iPhone. Both devices need to have Wi-Fi turned on and be signed in to the same iCloud account. On your Mac, select **FaceTime** > **Preferences** from the FaceTime menu and check On **Calls from iPhone** (from the Settings tab). On your iPhone, access **Settings** > **Phone** > **Calls on Other Devices** and drag the **Allow Calls on Other Devices** to **On**, and select a device under the **Allow Calls On** section.

1 Click on this icon on the Dock

2 You need an Apple ID to use FaceTime. Click here to enter the name, email address or cell number of the person you want to contact. Click on the video icon to make the call

3 When a call is connected, the other person's video feed is in the main window and your own is shown as a thumbnail

Hot tip

When a call is connected, click on this button and click on the **Add Person** button to add someone else to the call and create a Group call.

4 Move the cursor over the FaceTime screen to access the control buttons for, from left to right: viewing the details panel; muting a call; ending a call; turning off your video feed; and making the window full-screen

8 Digital Lifestyle

Leisure time, and how we use it, is a significant issue for everyone. This chapter details some of the options with macOS Catalina, including photos, music, movies and books.

Using the Photos App

The Photos app is designed to mirror the one used on iOS devices and integrate more with iCloud, so that you can store all of your photos in the iCloud and then view and manage them on all of your Apple devices.

If you are using the Photos app, you can specify how it operates with iCloud in its Preferences:

1 Open the Photos app and click on **Photos > Preferences** on the top toolbar

2 Click on the **General** button to apply settings for items including how Memories are displayed, how items are imported and whether videos and animated photos are played automatically

Don't forget

The iCloud options for the Photos app are: **iCloud Photos**, which uploads your entire photo library to the iCloud; and **Shared Albums**, which enables you to share photos from the Photos app with family and friends.

3 Click on the **iCloud** button for settings for using iCloud with the Photos app

Viewing Photos

The Photos app can be used to view photos according to years, months, days or at full size. This enables you to view your photos according to dates and times at which they were taken.

1 Click on the **Photos** button in the left-hand sidebar to the various categories for viewing photos

2 Click on the **All Photos** button on the top toolbar and select options for viewing photos

3 For each category, e.g. Months, the photos are displayed with the photos collated in easily-accessible formats

When you first open the Photos app you can select current photo libraries to import. This will ensure that all of the photos you want are available in the Photos app when you start.

Photos can be imported into the Photos app by selecting
File > **Import**
from the Menu bar and navigating to the required location within the Finder. This can be used to import photos from your Mac or an external device connected with an USB cable, such as a digital camera, a card reader or a flashdrive.

...cont'd

Drag this slider to change the magnification of the photo, or photos, being displayed, in Days, or All Photos view.

4 Double-click on a photo in the All Photos, Days or Months section to view it at full size

Hot tip

Click on the **Memories** button in the sidebar to view collections of related photos that have been collated by the Photos app, based on date and the best photos. Double-click on a Memory to view the photos within it. Click on this button in the bottom right-hand corner to view a Memory as a slideshow, with music and themes for transitions between each photo.

5 For a photo being displayed at full size use these buttons, from left to right, to: view information about it; share the photo; add it as a favorite; rotate it; apply auto-enhancement; and edit it

6 Click on the **Memories** button in the left-hand sidebar. This displays photos collated from specific dates (see Hot tip)

Using the sidebar

In the Photos app with macOS Catalina the sidebar at the left-hand side is permanently available regardless of the view being used; e.g. if you are looking at a Memory, or a photo at full size, the sidebar will still be available. To view categories and items in the sidebar:

1 Click on a category in the sidebar to view the items in the main window

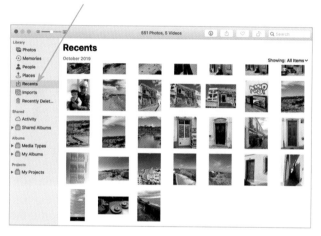

Hot tip

Click on the **People** or **Places** button in the sidebar to view collections of photos of specific people (based on the results of the Photos app scanning all of the available photos and identifying people within them) or locations where photos have been taken.

2 The sidebar categories have their own toolbar at the top of the window. For instance, the **Places** category shows locations at which photos have been taken, and this can be viewed as a **Map**, **Satellite** or **Grid**

Editing Photos

The Photos app has a range of editing options that can be used to enhance your photos. To do this:

1 Open a photo at full size

2 Click on the **Edit** button Edit

3 The main editing options are accessed from the **Adjust**, **Filters** and **Crop** buttons at the top of the window. Click on one of these to access its options in the right-hand panel

Don't forget

Click on the **Done** button at the top of the Photos app window to apply any editing changes that have been made.

4 For the **Adjust** options there is a slider that can be used to apply the amount of the required effect

5 The **Adjust** options also have an **Options** section that can be used to fine-tune the editing effects, such as by dragging the markers at the bottom of the Levels graph

6 Click on the **Filters** button to access preset filters that can be applied to the photo. Click on a filter to view the effect in the photo

7 Click on the **Crop** button to crop the photo by dragging the corner markers. Drag on the dial to the right of the photo to rotate it

8 Click on the **Done** button to apply the effects

Hot tip

In the Photos app with macOS Catalina, Live Photos can also be edited. These are short, animated photos that can be captured on an iPhone or an iPad, using iOS 10 or later.

The dedicated Music app is a new feature in macOS Catalina.

By default, songs are stored in the iTunes Library and streamed over Wi-Fi to play them on your Mac. However, they can also be downloaded to your Mac by tapping on this button, so that they can be played at any time, even when you are offline.

Never import music and use it for commercial purposes as this would be a breach of copyright.

Starting with the Music App

Music is a major part of the Apple ecosystem, and for many years iTunes has been integral to this. However, in macOS Catalina, the iTunes app has been removed and replaced with a dedicated Music app. (Other forms of media content – e.g. movies and TV shows – also now have their own dedicated apps – e.g. the TV app or the Podcast app.) To use the Music app:

1 Click on the **Music** app on the Dock

2 Under the **Library** heading in the left-hand sidebar, click on a category to view the available songs; e.g. by **Artists**

3 Click on a song or artist to view specific songs. Click on one to play it

4 Use these controls to, from left to right: shuffle songs, play previous, play/pause, play next and repeat

5 Drag this slider to change the volume

6 Click on the **iTunes Store** button in the left-hand sidebar to access the online store for buying more music

Although iTunes is no longer a separate app in macOS Catalina, the iTunes Store is still available from the Music app. This now just contains music, rather than the variety of content that was previously available in the iTunes Store. Once items have been bought, they are available in the Music app, as shown in Step 2 on the previous page.

7 Navigate around the iTunes Store Homepage using the panels and sections within the Homepage. Click here to access different music categories

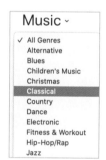

151

8 Click on a specific artist or album to view the available tracks. Click here to buy a whole album or click on individual songs to buy them

Never use illegal music or video download sites. Apart from the legal factor, they are much more likely to contain viruses and spyware.

Using Apple Music

Apple Music is a service that makes the entire Apple Music library of music available to users. It is a subscription service, and music can be streamed over the internet or downloaded so you can listen to it when you are offline. To start with Apple Music:

Numerous radio stations can also be listened to with Apple Music, including Beats 1.

1 Click on the **Music** app on the Dock

2 Click on the **For You** button on the top toolbar

3 Click on the **Try It Free** button to select for a free 3-month trial of the service

Discover new music every day.

Get playlists and albums inspired by the artists and genres you're listening to. 3 months free, then £9.99/month.

Try It Free

Learn More >

To end your Apple Music subscription at any point, open **Music** > **iTunes Store** and select **Account** > **View My Account** from the Menu bar. Log in with your Apple ID and in the **Account Information** window, under **Settings** click on the **Subscriptions** > **Manage** button. Click on the **Edit** button and drag the **Automatic Renewal** button to **Off**. You can then renew your Apple Music membership, if required, by selecting one of the **Options**.

4 After the trial period has expired, click on the required plan and click on the **Join Apple Music** button

Choose a plan

Individual
£9.99/month ✓

Family Up to 6 people
£14.99/month

University Student
£4.99/month

Plan automatically renews monthly until cancelled.

Join Apple Music

Not Now

Apple TV

Apple TV is an online service for downloading movies and TV shows. These were previously accessed from the iTunes app. Content can be bought or rented, depending on the item, and there is also access to the subscription TV service, Apple TV+. The content from Apple TV is accessed from the TV app:

1   Click on the **TV** app on the Dock

2   The initial content is displayed in the **Watch Now** window, with recommended content

3   Use these buttons on the top toolbar to access more content, including **Movies**, **TV Shows** and **Kids**

Watch Now	Movies	TV Shows	Kids	Library

4   Movies and TV shows can be accessed from their relevant categories. Details are displayed and, for some items, a preview is

available. Click on the **Buy** or **Rent** buttons as required

The dedicated TV app is a new feature in macOS Catalina.

Apple TV+ can also be accessed from the TV app. This is a monthly subscription service that provides exclusive movies and TV shows, created by Apple.

Hot tip

Click on the **Library** button on the top toolbar to view movies and TV shows that you have downloaded with the TV app.

Don't forget

If you rent a movie from the Apple TV Store, you have 30 days to watch it and 48 hours to complete it once you have started watching it.

Podcasts

Podcasts are becoming increasingly widespread and are a popular way to consume a wide range of audio content, covering topics including news, sport and comedy. macOS Catalina uses the Podcasts app to provide access to a vast library of podcasts:

The dedicated Podcasts app is a new feature in macOS Catalina.

Most podcasts consist of regular episodes, usually weekly. Once you have subscribed to a podcast, each episode will be downloaded as it is released. To play a podcast, click on the **Shows** button in the left-hand sidebar and click on the **Play Episode** button.

▶ Play Episode

1 Click on the **Podcasts** app on the Dock

2 Click on the **Browse** button in the left-hand sidebar and swipe up and down to view the available podcasts

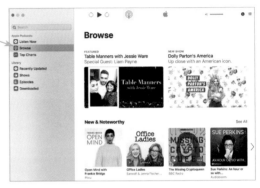

3 Click on a podcast to view its details. Click on the **Subscribe** button to subscribe to the podcast so that new episodes will be downloaded automatically

4 Click on these buttons in the left-hand sidebar to access more items in the Podcasts app

5 Click on these buttons in the left-hand sidebar to view the podcasts that you have subscribed to, including the overall show and individual episodes

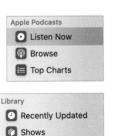

Reading with Books

Books is an eBook reading app that has been available with Apple's mobile devices, including the iPhone and the iPad, for a number of years. macOS Catalina also offers this technology for desktop and laptop Macs. To use Books:

1. Click on the **Books** app on the Dock and sign in with your Apple ID

2. All of the currently-available books are displayed in the **Library**

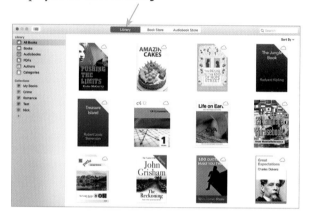

3. Click on the **Book Store** button to download more books

4. Click on a title to preview details about it

Books consists of your own library for storing and reading eBooks and also access to the online **Books Store** for buying and downloading new books. Items that you have downloaded with Books on other devices will also be available in your Books Library on your Mac.

Use these buttons in the sidebar of the Books Store to view books by **Featured**, **Top Charts**, **Categories** and **Top Authors**.

...cont'd

From the Books Store, click on the **Library** button on the top toolbar to go back to your own Library.

Use these buttons on the top toolbar of a book to, from left to right: go back to your Library; view the table of contents; or view any notes you have added.

Use these buttons on the top toolbar to, from left to right: change the text size; search for text; and add a bookmark to a page.

5. Click here to download the book (if it is a paid-for title this button will display a price)

6. The title will be downloaded into your Books Library. Double-click on the cover to open the book and start reading

7. Click or tap on the right-hand and left-hand edges to turn a page. Move the cursor over the top of the page to access the top toolbar. The bottom toolbar displays the page numbers and location

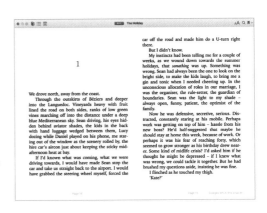

9 Sharing macOS

This chapter looks at how to set up and manage different user accounts on your Mac.

Adding Users

macOS enables multiple users to access individual accounts on the same computer. If there are multiple users (i.e. two or more for a single machine), each person can log in individually and access their own files and folders. This means that each person can log in to their own settings and preferences. All user accounts can be password-protected, to ensure that each user's environment is secure. To set up multiple user accounts:

Don't forget

Every computer with multiple users has at least one main user, also known as the administrator. This means that they have greater control over the number of items that they can edit and alter. If there is only one user on a computer, they automatically take on the role of the administrator. Administrators have a particularly important role to play when computers are networked together. Each computer can potentially have several administrators.

1 Click on the **System Preferences** icon on the Dock

2 Click on the **Users & Groups** icon

Users & Groups

3 The information about the current user account is displayed. This is your own account, and the information is based on details you provided when you first set up your Mac

Don't forget

Each user can select their own icon or photo of themselves.

4 Click on this icon to enter your password to unlock the settings so that new accounts can be added

Click the lock to prevent further changes.

5 Click on the **+** button to add a new account

6 Enter the details for the new account holder

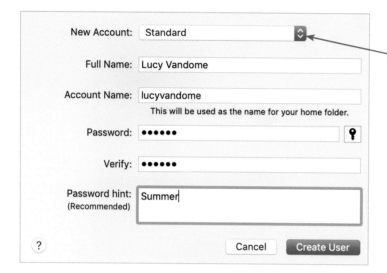

New Account:	Standard
Full Name:	Lucy Vandome
Account Name:	lucyvandome
	This will be used as the name for your home folder.
Password:	●●●●●●
Verify:	●●●●●●
Password hint: (Recommended)	Summer

?   Cancel   Create User

Don't forget

At Step 6, choose the type of account from the drop-down list. An **Administrator** account is one that allows the user to make system changes, and add or delete other users. A **Standard** account allows the user to use the functionality of the Mac, but not change system settings. **Sharing Only** is an account that allows guests to log in temporarily, without a password – when they log out, all files and information will be deleted from the guest account.

7 Click on the **Create User** button

8 The new account is added to the list in the Users & Groups window, under **Other Users**

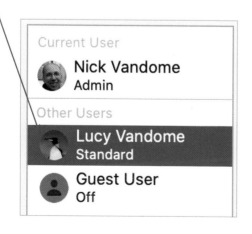

Current User

Nick Vandome
Admin

Other Users

Lucy Vandome
Standard

Guest User
Off

Don't forget

By default, you are the administrator of your own Mac. This means that you can administer other user accounts.

Deleting Users

Once a user has been added, their name appears on the list in the Users & Groups dialog box (see Step 8 on the previous page). It is then possible to edit the details of the particular user or delete them altogether. To do this:

Beware

Always tell other users if you are planning to delete them from the system. Don't just remove them and then let them find out the next time they try to log in. If you delete a user, their personal files are left untouched and can still be accessed, if you select **Don't change the home folder** in Step 3.

1 Within **Users & Groups**, unlock the settings as shown in Step 4 on page 158, then select a user from the list

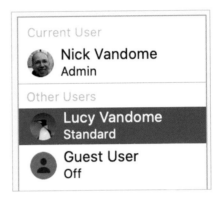

2 Click here to remove the selected person's user account

3 A warning box appears, to check if you really do want to delete the selected user. If you do, select the required option and click on the **Delete User** button

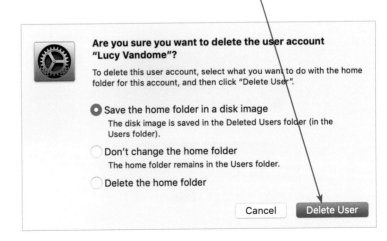

Fast User Switching

If there are multiple users on your macOS system, it is useful to be able to switch between them as quickly as possible. When this is done, the first user's session is retained so that they can return to it if required. To switch between users:

Don't forget

Unlock the settings before you start (see Step 4 on page 158).

1 In the Users & Groups window, click on the **Login Options** button

2 Check **On** the **Show fast user switching menu as** box, then close the window

Don't forget

When you switch between users, the first user remains logged in, and their current session remains intact.

3 At the top right of the screen, click on the current user's name

Nick Vandome

4 Click on the name of another user

Don't forget

Users can sign in from the Lock screen with a password by clicking on their own icon/name on the screen and entering the relevant details. If fast user switching is not used, each user has to log out before the next one can sign in.

5 Enter the relevant password (if required)

Lucy Vandome

6 Click on this button to log in

161

Screen Time

The amount of time that we spend on our digital devices is a growing issue in society, and steps are being taken to let us see exactly how much time we are spending looking at our computer screens. In macOS Catalina, a range of screen-use options can be monitored with the Screen Time feature. To use this:

Screen Time is a new feature in macOS Catalina.

1 Select **System Preferences** > **Screen Time**

Screen Time

2 Click on the **Options** button

Options

3 Click on the **Turn On...** button to activate Screen Time

Screen Time for this Mac: Off   Turn On...

☐ Share across devices
You can enable this on any iPhone, iPad, or Mac signed in to iCloud to report your combined screen time.

☐ Use Screen Time Passcode
Use a passcode to secure Screen Time settings, and to allow for more time when limits expire.

Don't forget

If Family Sharing has been set up (see pages 46-51) it can be used to monitor the screen time of other Family Sharing members; e.g. children. To do this, click on the **Screen Time** button in **System Preferences > Family Sharing**.

Screen Time

4 Click on the **App Usage** button in the left-hand sidebar to view the overall screen usage. Click here to select a different time period to view

App Usage

Downtime

This can be used to specify times when the computer and its apps cannot be accessed:

1 Check **On** the **Every Day** button to apply time limits for a whole week

2 Check **On** the **Custom** button to apply time limits for individual days

App Limits

This can be used to limit the amount of time that certain categories of apps can be accessed:

1 Click on the **+** button at the bottom of the **App Limits** window

2 Click on any category to which you want limits to apply

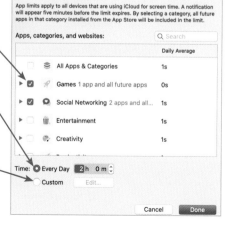

3 Click here to set a time limit for the categories selected in Step 2. Click on the **Custom** option to apply custom times as for Downtime

All of the Screen Time options can be accessed from the left-hand sidebar of the main window.

In general, the categories for app limits relate to the categories under which the apps are listed in the App Store.

...cont'd

Always Allowed

This can be used to allow the use of specified apps, regardless of other settings:

Check **On** the items that you want to allow, regardless of any other Screen Time settings

Don't forget

Click on the **Stores** button under **Content & Privacy** to access options for content that is downloaded from the App Store, the Music app, the TV app and the Podcasts app. Selections can be made for age-appropriate content and also blocking content with explicit language. Click on the **Apps** button to allow the use of specific apps regardless of other privacy restrictions.

Content & Privacy

This can be used to add restrictions based on the type of content being viewed:

Click on the **Content** tab to restrict content based on criteria such as adult content and explicit language

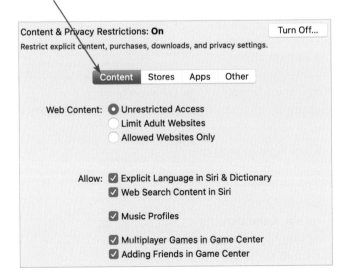

10 Networking

This chapter looks at networking and how to share files over a network.

Networking Overview

Before you start sharing files directly between computers, you have to connect them together. This is known as networking and can be done with two computers in the same room, or with thousands of computers in a major corporation. If you are setting up your own small network, it will be known in the computing world as a Local Area Network (LAN). When setting up a network there are various pieces of hardware that are initially required to join all of the network items together. Once this has been done, software settings can be applied for the networked items. Some of the items of hardware that may be required include:

- **A network card**. This is known as a Network Interface Card (NIC), and all recent Macs have them built in.

- **A wireless router**. This is for a wireless network, which is increasingly the most common way to create a network via Wi-Fi. The router is connected to a telephone line and the computer then communicates with it wirelessly.

- **An Ethernet port and Ethernet cable**. This enables you to make the physical connection between devices. Ethernet cables come in a variety of forms, but the one you should be looking for is the Cat6 type as this allows for the fastest transfer of data. If you are creating a wireless network then you will not require these.

- **A hub**. This is a piece of hardware with multiple Ethernet ports that enables you to connect all of your devices together and lets them communicate with each other. However, conflicts can occur with hubs if two devices try to send data through one at the same time.

- **A switch**. This is similar in operation to a hub but it is more sophisticated in its method of data transfer, thus allowing all of the machines on the network to communicate simultaneously, unlike a hub.

Once you have worked out all of the devices that you want to include on your network, you can arrange them accordingly. Try to keep the switches and hub within relative proximity of a power supply and if you are using cables, make sure they are laid out safely.

Don't forget

Connecting to the internet is also another form of network connection.

Beware

The latest models of the MacBook Pro do not have a separate Ethernet port. However, a Thunderbolt to Ethernet adapter can be used to connect an Ethernet cable to a MacBook Pro.

Ethernet network

The cheapest and easiest way to network computers is to create an Ethernet network. This involves buying an Ethernet hub or switch, which enables you to connect several devices to a central point; i.e. the hub or switch. All Apple computers and most modern printers have an Ethernet connection, so it is possible to connect various devices, not just computers. Once all of the devices have been connected by Ethernet cables, you can then start applying network settings.

AirPort network

Another option for creating a network is using Apple's own wireless system, AirPort. This creates a wireless network, and there are two main options used by Apple computers: AirPort Express, using the IEEE 802.11n standard, which is more commonly known as Wi-Fi; and the newer AirPort Extreme, using the next-generation IEEE 802.11ac standard, which is up to five times faster than the 802.11n standard. Thankfully, AirPort Express and Extreme are also compatible with devices based on the older IEEE standards, 802.11a/b/g/n, so one machine loaded with AirPort Extreme can still communicate wirelessly with the older AirPort version.

One of the main issues with a wireless network is security, since it is possible for someone with a wireless-enabled machine to access your wireless network if they are within range. However, in the majority of cases the chances of this happening are fairly slim, although it is an issue about which you should be aware.

The basic components of a wireless network between Macs are an AirPort card (either AirPort Express or AirPort Extreme) installed in all of the required machines, and an AirPort base station that can be located anywhere within 150 meters of the AirPort-enabled computers. Once the hardware is in place, wireless-enabled devices can be configured using the AirPort Utility setup assistant found in the Utilities/Other folder. After AirPort has been set up, the wireless network can be connected. All of the wireless-enabled devices should then be able to communicate with each other, without the use of a multitude of cables.

Wireless network

A wireless network can also be created with a standard wireless router, rather than using the AirPort option.

Another method for connecting items wirelessly is Bluetooth. This covers much shorter distances than AirPort, and is usually used for items such as printers and smartphones. Bluetooth devices can be connected using the Bluetooth File Exchange utility: select the required files you want to exchange via Bluetooth and then select the required device.

AirPort Time Capsule is a method of backing up, using Wi-Fi instead of a cable connection. It offers up to 3TB of storage and is designed to work with Time Machine (see pages 174-177).

Network Settings

Once you have connected the hardware needed for a network, you can start applying the network settings that are required for connecting to the internet, for online access.

1 In **System Preferences**, click on the **Network** button

Network

2 For a wireless connection, click on the **Turn Wi-Fi On** button

Turn Wi-Fi On

3 Details of wireless settings are displayed

Hot tip

An Ethernet cable can be used to connect to a router instead of using a Wi-Fi connection, and it can also be used to connect two computers.

4 For a cable connection, connect an Ethernet cable (via an adapter in the Thunderbolt port) and click on the **Thunderbolt** option

5 Click on the **Advanced...** button to see the full settings for each option

Advanced...

File Sharing

One of the main reasons for creating a network of two or more computers is to share files between them. On networked Macs, this involves setting them up so that they can share files, and then accessing these files.

Setting up file sharing

To set up file sharing on a networked Mac:

1 Click on the **System Preferences** button on the Dock

2 Click on the **Sharing** icon

Sharing

3 Check **On** the boxes next to the items you want to share (the most common items to share are files and printers)

On	Service
☐	Screen Sharing
✓	File Sharing
☐	Media Sharing
✓	Printer Sharing
☐	Remote Login
☐	Remote Management
☐	Remote Apple Events
☐	Internet Sharing
✓	Bluetooth Sharing
☐	Content Caching

Hot tip

For macOS users, files can also be shared with the AirDrop option. This can be used with two Macs, and compatible iPhones and iPads that have this facility. Files can be shared simply by dragging them onto the icon of the other user that appears in the AirDrop window. To access AirDrop, click on this button in the Finder.

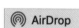

AirDrop

Connecting to a Network

Connecting as a registered user

To connect as a registered user (usually as yourself when you want to access items on another one of your own computers):

Don't forget

The username and password used to connect to a networked computer as a registered user are the ones used to log in to your Mac. There is also an option to connect using your Apple ID.

1 Click on the **Network** button on the Finder sidebar

2 Click on the networked computer to which you want to connect

3 Click on the **Connect As...** button

Connect As...

4 Check On the **Registered User** button, and enter your username and password

5 Click on the **Connect** button

6 The public folders and home folder of the networked computer are available to the registered user. Double-click on an item to view its contents

Don't forget

You can disconnect from a networked computer by ejecting it in the Finder in the same way as you would for a removable drive, such as a flashdrive (see page 53) by clicking on the eject button.

Guest users

Guest users on a network are users other than yourself or other registered users, to whom you want to limit access to your files and folders. Guests only have access to a folder called the Drop Box in your own Public folder. To share files with guest users you have to first copy them into the Drop Box. To do this:

1 Create a file and select **File** > **Save** from the Menu bar

2 Navigate to your own home folder (this is created automatically by macOS and displayed in the Finder sidebar with your Mac username)

3 Double-click on the **Public** folder

Public

4 Double-click on the **Drop Box** folder

Shared Folder

Drop Box

5 Save the file into the Drop Box

Shared Folder

026.JPG

Beware

If another user is having problems accessing the files in your Drop Box, check the Permissions settings that have been assigned to the files. See page 186 for further details.

Hot tip

The contents of the Drop Box can be accessed by other users on the same computer as well as users on the network.

Beware

The Drop Box folder is not the same as the Dropbox app, which is used for online storage and backing up.

172

...cont'd

Accessing a Drop Box

To access files in a Drop Box:

1 Access a networked computer as shown on page 170

2 Click on the **Connect As...** button in the Finder window

3 Check On the **Guest** button

Enter your name and password for the server "Eilidh's MacBook Pro".

Connect As: ● Guest
○ Registered User
○ Using an Apple ID

Cancel   Connect

4 Click on the **Connect** button

5 Double-click on a user's **Public Folder**

Nick Vandome's Public Folder

6 Double-click on the **Drop Box** folder to access the files within it

Drop Box

Beware

It is better to copy files into the Drop Box rather than moving them completely from their primary location.

Hot tip

Set permissions for how the Drop Box operates by selecting it in the Finder and **Ctrl + clicking** on it. Select **Get Info** from the menu, and apply the required settings under the **Sharing & Permissions** heading.

11 Maintaining macOS

Despite its stability, macOS still benefits from a robust maintenance regime. This chapter looks at ways to keep macOS in top shape and ensure apps are as secure as possible, and looks at some general troubleshooting.

Time Machine

Time Machine is a feature of macOS that gives you great peace of mind. In conjunction with an external hard drive it creates a backup of your whole system, including folders, files, apps, and even the macOS operating system itself.

Once it has been set up, Time Machine takes a backup every hour, and you can then go into Time Machine to restore any files that have been deleted or become corrupt since the last backup.

Setting up Time Machine

To use Time Machine, it first has to be set up. This involves attaching a hard drive to your Mac via cable or wirelessly, depending on the type of hard drive you have. To set up Time Machine:

Beware

Make sure that you have an external hard drive that is larger than the contents of your Mac, otherwise Time Machine will not be able to back it all up.

Don't forget

The hard drive must be connected in order to use Time Machine. Or, you could use AirPort Time Capsule, which is a method of backing up using Wi-Fi instead of a cable connection. It offers up to 3TB of storage and is designed to work with Time Machine.

1 Click on the **Time Machine** icon in System Preferences

Time Machine

2 In the Time Machine window, click on the **Select Disk...** button

Select Disk...

Time Machine

Time Machine
13.7 GB of 250 GB available
Oldest backup: October 29, 2018
Latest backup: October 29, 2018
Next backup: When disk is connected

Select Disk...

Time Machine
☑ Back Up Automatically

Time Machine keeps:
• Local snapshots as space permits
• Hourly backups for the past 24 hours
• Daily backups for the past month
• Weekly backups for all previous months
The oldest backups are deleted when your disk becomes full.

☑ Show Time Machine in menu bar   Options... ?

3 Connect an external hard drive and select it from the list

4 Click on the **Use Disk** button

5 In the Time Machine window, check **On** the **Back Up Automatically** option

6 The backup will begin. The initial backup copies your whole system and can take several hours. Subsequent hourly backups only look at items that have been changed since the previous backup

7 The record of backups and the schedule for the next one are shown here

Beware

When you first set up Time Machine it copies everything on your Mac. Depending on the type of connection you have for your external drive, this could take several hours. Because of this, it is a good idea to have a hard drive with a USB 3.0 or Thunderbolt connection to make it as fast as possible.

175

Don't forget

If you stop the initial backup before it has been completed, Time Machine will remember where it has stopped and resume the backup from this point.

...cont'd

Using Time Machine

Once Time Machine has been set up, it can then be used to go back in time to view items in an earlier state. To do this:

If you have deleted items before the initial setup of Time Machine, these will not be recoverable.

1 Access an item on your Mac and delete it. In this example, the folder **Time Machine 1** has been deleted

2 Click on the **Time Machine** icon

3 Time Machine displays the selected window in its current state (the Time Machine 1 folder is deleted). Earlier versions are stacked behind it

Don't forget

The active item that you were viewing before you launched Time Machine is the one that is active in the Time Machine interface. You can select items from within the active window to view their contents.

4 Click on the arrows to move through the open items, or select a time or date from the scale to the right of the arrows

5 Another way to move through Time Machine is to click on the pages behind the first one. This brings the selected item to the front

6 Move back through the windows to find the deleted item. Click on it and click on the **Restore** button to restore the item, in this case the **Time Machine 1** folder

Don't forget

Items are restored from the Time Machine backup disk; i.e. the external hard drive.

7 Click on the **Cancel** button to return to your normal environment, without restoring the item

Cancel

8 The deleted folder **Time Machine 1** is now restored to its original location

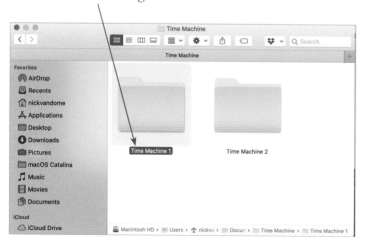

Disk Utility

Disk Utility is a utility app that allows you to perform certain testing and repair functions for macOS. It incorporates a variety of functions, and is a good option for both general maintenance and if your computer is not running as it should.

Each of the functions within Disk Utility can be applied to specific drives and volumes. However, it is not possible to use the macOS start-up disk within Disk Utility as this will be in operation to run the app, and Disk Utility cannot operate on a disk that has apps already running. To use Disk Utility:

Checking disks

Don't forget

Disk Utility is located within the **Applications** > **Utilities (Other)** folder.

Disk Utility

1 Open Disk Utility then click the **First Aid** tab to check a disk

2 Select a disk and select one of the First Aid options

Erasing a disk
To erase all of the data on a disk or a volume:

Don't forget

If there is a problem with a disk and macOS can fix it, the **Repair** button will be available. Click on this to enable Disk Utility to repair the problem.

1 Click on the **Erase** tab, and select a disk or a volume

Beware

If you erase data from a removable disk such as a flashdrive, you will not be able to retrieve it.

2 Click **Erase** to erase the data on the selected disk or volume

Erase

System Information

This can be used to view how the different hardware and software elements on your Mac are performing. To do this:

1 Open the **Utilities** folder and double-click on the **System Information** icon

2 Click on the **Hardware** link and click on an item of hardware

System Information is located within the **Applications** > **Utilities (Other)** folder.

3 Details about the item of hardware, and its performance, are displayed

4 Similarly, click on network or software items to view their details

Activity Monitor

Activity Monitor is a utility app that can be used to view information about how much processing power and memory is being used to run apps. This can be useful to know if certain apps are running slowly or crashing frequently. To use Activity Monitor:

Activity Monitor is located within the **Applications** > **Utilities (Other)** folder.

Activity Monitor

1 Open the Activity Monitor and click on the **CPU** tab to see how much processor capacity is being used up

System:	9.71%	CPU LOAD	Threads:	1674
User:	9.26%		Processes:	474
Idle:	81.03%			

2 Click on the **Memory** tab to see how much system memory (RAM) is being used up

MEMORY PRESSURE	Physical Memory:	8.00 GB	App Memory:	3.62 GB
	Memory Used:	6.72 GB	Wired Memory:	2.32 GB
	Cached Files:	1.26 GB	Compressed:	803.6 MB
	Swap Used:	924.5 MB		

3 Click on the **Energy** tab to see details of battery usage (for a laptop)

ENERGY IMPACT		BATTERY (Last 12 hours)
Remaining charge:	85%	
Time remaining:	2:53	
Time on battery:	1:39	

4 Click on the **Disk** tab to see how much space has been taken up on the hard drive

Reads in:	1,855,066	IO	Data read:	39.27 GB
Writes out:	1,850,509		Data written:	41.86 GB
Reads in/sec:	229		Data read/sec:	1.17 MB
Writes out/sec:	198		Data written/sec:	3.33 MB

Updating Software

Apple periodically releases updates for its software; both its apps and the macOS operating system. All of these are now available through the App Store. To update software:

1 Open **System Preferences** and click on the **Software Update** icon

Software Update

2 Click on the **Advanced...** button

Advanced...

3 Make selections here for how you are notified about updates and how they are downloaded

Automatically:
- ☑ Check for updates
- ☑ Download new updates when available
- ☐ Install macOS updates
- ☐ Install app updates from the App Store

- ☑ Install system data files and security updates

OK

4 Available updates are shown in the **Updates** section of the App Store. Click on the **Update**

⬇ Updates

buttons to update. If there are no updates available this will be stated, with the latest updates underneath

Updates   Update All

Pending

Numbers
Yesterday   UPDATE

Keynote
Yesterday   UPDATE

This update contains stability and performance improvements.   more

This update contains stability and performance improvements.   more

iMovie
Yesterday   UPDATE

Agenda – A new take on notes
Oct 30, 2018   UPDATE

What's New in Version 10.1.10
• Removes the option to share video files more

NEW
- It is now possible to edit the displayed d more

Hot tip

Software updates can also be accessed directly from the Apple menu, located on the top Menu bar. If updates are available this is denoted on the **App Store** link on the Apple menu, or on the App Store app's icon.

Don't forget

For some software updates, such as those for the macOS itself, you may have to restart your computer for them to take effect.

Gatekeeper

Internet security is an important issue for every computer user; no-one wants their computer to be infected with a virus or malicious software. Historically, Macs have been less prone to attack from viruses than Windows-based machines, but this does not mean Mac users can be complacent. With their increasing popularity there is now more temptation for virus writers to target them. macOS Catalina recognizes this, and has taken steps to prevent attacks with the Gatekeeper function. To use this:

1 Open **System Preferences** and click on the **Security & Privacy** icon

Security & Privacy

2 Click on the **General** tab   General

3 Click on one of these buttons to determine which location apps can be downloaded from. You can select from just the Mac App Store, or Mac App Store and identified developers, which gives you added security in terms of apps having been thoroughly checked

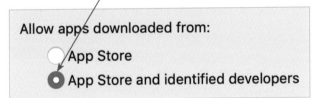

Allow apps downloaded from:
- App Store
- App Store and identified developers

4 Under the **General** tab there are also options for using a password when you log in to your account; if a password is required after sleep or if the screen saver is activated; showing a message when the screen is locked; or allowing your Apple Watch to unlock your Mac

General FileVault Firewall Privacy

A login password has been set for this user   Change Password...

☑ Require password 5 minutes ⬍ after sleep or screen saver begins

☐ Show a message when the screen is locked   Set Lock Message...

☑ Allow your Apple Watch to unlock your Mac

Privacy

Also within the Security & Privacy System Preferences are options for activating a firewall and privacy settings. To access these:

1 Click on the **Firewall** tab

Firewall

2 Click on the **Turn On Firewall** button to activate this. Click on **Firewall Options...** to change settings for the firewall

A firewall is an application that aims to stop malicious software from accessing your computer.

3 Click on the **Privacy** tab

Privacy

4 Click on the **Location Services** link and check **On** the **Enable Location Services** option if you want relevant apps to be able to access your location

5 Click on the **Contacts** link and check **On** any relevant apps that are allowed to access your contacts

6 Click on the **Analytics & Improvements** link and check **On** or **Off** the options for sharing analytical information with Apple and app developers. This will include any problems, and helps Apple improve its software and apps. This information is collected anonymously

Problems with Apps

The simple answer

macOS is something of a rarity in the world of computing software: it claims to be remarkably stable, and it is. However, this is not to say that things do not sometimes go wrong, although this is considerably less frequent than with older Mac operating systems. Sometimes this will be due to problems within particular apps, and on occasions the problems may lie with macOS itself. If this does happen, the first course of action is to restart macOS using the **Apple menu > Restart...** command. If this does not work, or you cannot access the Restart command as the Mac has frozen, try turning off the power to the computer and then starting up again.

Force quitting

If a particular app is not responding, it can be closed down separately without the need to reboot the computer. To do this:

When there are updates to macOS, these can on rare occasions cause issues with some apps. However, these are usually fixed with subsequent patches and upgrades to macOS.

1 Select **Apple menu > Force Quit...** from the Menu bar

2 Select the app you want to close

3 Click the **Force Quit** button

General Troubleshooting

It is true that things do occasionally go wrong with macOS, although probably with less regularity than with some other operating systems. If something does go wrong, there are a number of areas that you can check and also some steps you can take to ensure that you do not lose any important data if the worst-case scenario occurs, and your hard drive packs up completely:

- **Backup**. If everything does go wrong it is essential that you have taken preventative action in the form of making sure that all of your data is backed up and saved. This can be done with either the Time Machine app or by backing up manually by copying data to a flashdrive. Some content is also automatically backed up if you have iCloud activated.

- **Reboot**. One traditional reply by IT helpdesks is to reboot (i.e. turn off the computer and turn it back on again) and hope that the problem has resolved itself. In a lot of cases this simple operation does the trick, but it is not always a viable solution for major problems.

- **Check cables**. If the problem appears to be with a network connection or an externally-connected device, check that all cables are connected properly and have not become loose. If possible, make sure that all cables are tucked away so that they cannot be inadvertently pulled out.

- **Check network settings**. If your network or internet connections are not working, check the network settings in System Preferences. Sometimes when you make a change to one item, this can have an adverse effect on one of these settings. (If possible, lock the settings once you have applied them by clicking on the padlock icon in the Network preferences window.)

- **Check for viruses**. If your computer is infected with a virus this could affect the efficient running of the machine. Luckily, this is less of a problem for Macs as virus writers tend to concentrate their efforts towards Windows-based machines. However, this is changing as Macs become more popular, and there are plenty of Mac viruses out there. So make sure your computer is protected by an app such as Norton AntiVirus, which is available from **www.norton.com**

Don't forget

In extreme cases, you will not be able to reboot your computer normally. If this happens, you will have to pull out the power cable and re-attach it. You will then be able to reboot, although the computer may want to check its hard drive to make sure that everything is in working order.

...cont'd

If you are having problems opening a document that you have been sent from a trusted source, contact them to make sure that the document has not been locked with a password. If you receive documents from someone you do not know, such as by email, do not open them as they may contain viruses or malware.

Within the Screen Saver System Preferences (Desktop & Screen Saver) is a button for **Hot Corners**. Click on this to access options for specifying what happens when the cursor is pointed over the four corners of the screen. This includes accessing the Notification Center and the Launchpad, or putting the Mac display to sleep.

● **Check start-up items**. If you have set certain items to start automatically when your computer is turned on, this could cause certain conflicts within your machine. If this is the case, disable the items from launching during the booting-up of the computer. This can be done within the Users & Groups section of System Preferences by clicking on the **Login Items** tab, selecting the relevant item and pressing the minus button.

● **Check permissions**. If you or other users are having problems opening items, this could be because of the permissions that are set. To check these, select the item in the Finder, click on the **File** button on the top Menu bar and select **Get Info**. In the **Sharing & Permissions** section of the Info window you will be able to set the relevant permissions to allow other users, or yourself, to read, write or have no access.

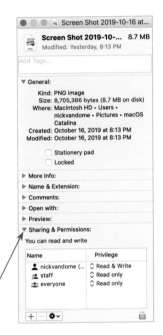

Click here to view Permissions settings

● **Eject external devices**. Sometimes external devices, such as flashdrives, can become temperamental and refuse to eject the disks within them, or even not show up on the Desktop or in the Finder at all. If this happens, you can try to eject the disk by pressing the mouse button when the Mac chimes are heard during the booting-up process.

● **Turn off your screen saver**. Screen savers can sometimes cause conflicts within your computer, particularly if they have been downloaded from an unreliable source. If this happens, change the screen saver within the **Screen Saver** tab in the **Desktop & Screen Saver** preference of the System Preferences, or disable it altogether.

Index

189